guitar

the easy chord  book

The Guide to Making Easy Chords Sound Great!

DAN DONNELLY

Alfred, the leader in educational publishing, and the National Guitar Workshop, one of America's finest guitar schools, have joined forces to bring you the best, most progressive educational tools possible. We hope you will enjoy this book and encourage you to look for other fine products from Alfred and the National Guitar Workshop.

This book was acquired, edited and produced by Workshop Arts, Inc., the publishing arm of the National Guitar Workshop.

Nathaniel Gunod, editor
Gary Tomassetti, music typesetter
Margo Farnsworth, chord illustrations
Timothy Phelps, interior design
CD recorded by Darrell Ashley at Studio 9, Pomona, CA

Guitar cover photos: Fender Musical Instruments, Inc. (Electric)
Martin Guitar Company (Acoustic)
Lightbulb photos: © PhotoDisc, Inc.

ISBN 0-7390-0798-X (Book)
ISBN 0-7390-0799-8 (Book & CD)
ISBN 0-7390-0800-5 (CD)

table of contents

about the author

Danny Donnelly is a Native Californian who works as a recording artist, singer/songwriter and studio guitarist in Los Angeles. Danny has over twenty years of experience as a guitarist in a wide variety of styles. He holds degrees in music from the University of Southern California and Long Beach City College.

Acknowledgements

The following gracious people have inspired and/or encouraged the subject matter and completion of this book: Nat Gunod; Jody Fisher and the National Guitar Workshop faculty; Martin Simpson; Eric Halbig; Tim Kobza; Frank Potenza; Jan Moorhead; Jake White; Rachel Harris; Amalcar; Todd Washington; the faculty and alumni friends from the USC Studio Jazz Guitar Department; Wayne Riker; David Wilcox; Peter Himmelman; David Hamburger; Pat Sandy; Debbie Donnelly; Pat Barnes; Danilo Galura; Jon Patriarca; Andy Abod; Scot Neraki; John Lightfoot; Christopher Williams; Adam Levy; Jon Turner; Sean Holt; Michael Donnelly; Roby LaPorte; Bob Dylan; Jeff LaPierre; Steve Remender; Richard Beckman; Paul Anderson; Jessi Alexander; Jack Pearson; Evan Hail; Steve Oraho; Chuck Broadsky; Michael Hedges and Willie Porter. Special thanks to the Lord for all of you and for the gift of music.

The charts on pages 20 and 21 were developed by Susan Mazer of the National Guitar Workshop.

Track 1

The CD that accompanies this book can make learning with the book easier and more enjoyable. The symbol shown above will appear next to every example that is on the CD. Use the CD to help insure that you are capturing the feel of the examples, interpreting the rhythms correctly, and so on. The track numbers below the symbols correspond directly to the examples on that page. Track 1 will help you tune your guitar to this CD.

introduction

As a guitar teacher, I have noticed that many students, from the novice to the advanced, ask similar questions about chords. This book was written in response to those questions. I saw the need for a book that would dig into the "street knowledge" of simple guitar chords: easy chord theory, sweet chord substitution ideas, embellishments for accompaniments, picking and strumming patterns, alternate tunings and many other topics.

This book assumes that you already play the guitar and have a basic knowledge of chords, hammer-ons, pull-offs and other basic techniques. There is a quick review of reading standard music notation and TAB, and other concepts are covered as the book continues. If you have gaps in your knowledge, these explanations will help you use the book.

The information in this book was acquired by studying the techniques of many great players the world over, as well as by personal trial and error. In order for you to use this information most efficiently, I suggest that you work on a small amount of material at a time. Whether you're a performing songwriter, a band member, an accompanist, a campfire strummer or just a weekend picker, you should grab a few ideas at a time and experiment with them for awhile before you come back for more.

This book contains lessons on:

- Easy ways to play "hard" chords.
- How to "spice up" open position chords you've played for years.
- How to play those chord embellishments you've heard on recordings for years but never knew how to play.
- The basic theory of chord progressions.
- An overview of chord families, or which chords go with which keys.
- How best to use a capo.
- Voice leading, or the movement of notes between chords.
- Fingerpicking patterns that will work well in your accompaniments.
- Strumming techniques and styles.
- Chord cadences, or "endings for songs."
- Hammer-on and pull-off licks within chords.
- A quick and easy (but still inspiring) introduction to alternate tunings.
- A guide for accompanists and songwriters.
- An introduction to blues ideas and slide technique.
- Several helpful tunes to play that put the techniques you learn to practical use.

> **NOTE:**
> This book is full of great ideas for players of all levels. There are hundreds of examples for strumming and picking. Although some of the music notation and chord diagrams may *look* difficult, they aren't. Just be patient as you look at each diagram. They are very detailed and descriptive. You'll find the playing is fun and easy. Enjoy!

CAGED

Make sure that you know the five chord forms* below before you get started. Together, the names of these chords form the word CAGED. These chord shapes will be fundamental to some ideas that will be covered in this book. Have fun!

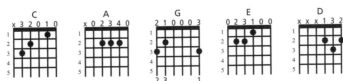

* For information on how to read these chords, see page 7.

review the basics

Standard Music Notation

Reading standard music notation is a necessary skill for anyone interested in becoming a better musician. Once you learn a few basic concepts, you'll find that reading music is really easy and a whole world of musical possibilities will open up for you. There are two basic elements to standard notation: *pitch* and *rhythm*. Every note has a particular name (pitch) and a particular duration (rhythm). The note's pitch is determined by the particular staff line or space on which it is positioned.

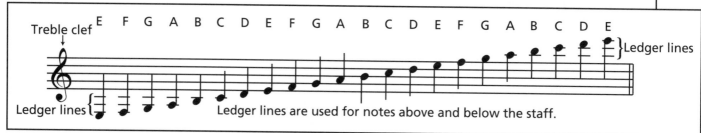

Every song has numbers at the beginning, called the *time signature*, that tell us how to count the time. The top number represents the number of beats or counts per *measure*. The bottom number represents the type of note receiving one beat or count. The most common time signature, $\frac{4}{4}$ is shown below. In $\frac{4}{4}$ time, there are four beats per measure and the quarter note (♩) receives one beat.

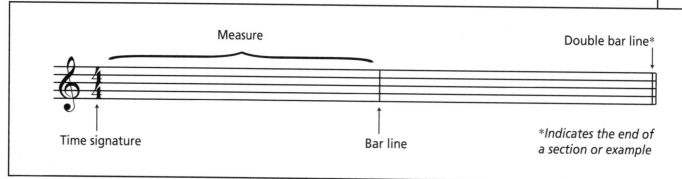

The appearance of the note—the type of note head or stem that it has—tells you its duration. Finally, rests tell you when and for how long *not* to play, which is also an important aspect of rhythm. Here are the note values in $\frac{4}{4}$ time:

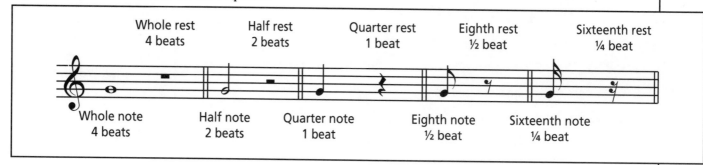

Tablature is a system of notation that graphically represents the strings and frets of the guitar fingerboard. Each note is indicated by placing a number, which indicates the fret to play, on the appropriate string.

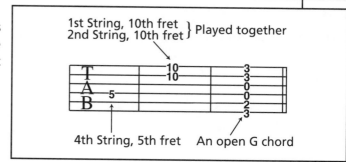

💡 The Chord Diagrams

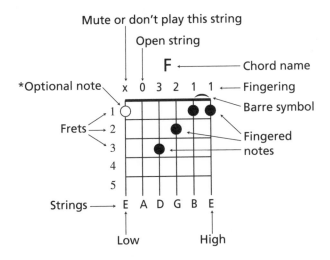

Mute or don't play this string

Open string

F — Chord name

*Optional note

Fingering

Barre symbol

Fingered notes

Frets

Strings — E A D G B E

Low   High

* If there is an optional note, you can play either note indicated on that string.

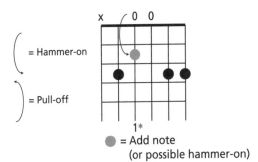

= Hammer-on

= Pull-off

= Add note (or possible hammer-on)

*Fingering numbers beneath diagrams apply to added or optional notes.

Multiple chord shapes on the same diagram are indicated by lines that connect the dots.

Open chord

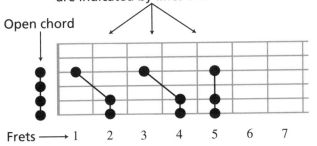

Frets — 1 2 3 4 5 6 7

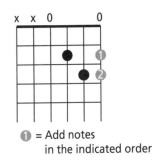

= Add notes in the indicated order

💡 TAB

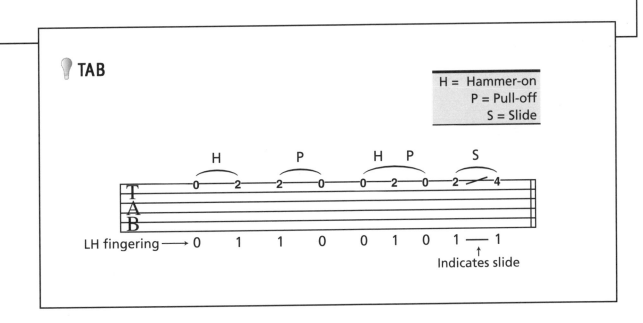

H = Hammer-on
P = Pull-off
S = Slide

LH fingering

Indicates slide

💡 Roman Numerals

In music, Roman numerals are used to indicate harmonies. Here's a quick review of Roman numerals, in upper and lowercase, and their Arabic equivalents:

I, i 1	II, ii 2	III, iii 3
IV, iv 4	V, v 5	VI, vi 6
	VII, vii ...7	

💡 The Major Scale

Half Steps and Whole Steps

The distance between any two notes is called an *interval*. The smallest interval is a *half step*, which is a distance of one fret. For example, the distance from the 1st fret to the 2nd fret is one half step. The distance of two half steps—two frets—is called a *whole step*. For example, the distance from the 1st fret to the 3rd is a whole step.

A *scale* is a series of notes arranged in a specific order of whole steps and half steps. The notes of a scale ascend in alphabetical order and descend in reverse alphabetical order (the musical alphabet consists of the first seven letters of the English alphabet, A through G). Each note in the scale is called a *scale degree*. The scale degrees are numbered upward from the lowest note.

A *major scale* is made up of eight notes with half steps between the 3rd and 4th and the 7th and 8th degrees. The rest are whole steps. The scale takes its name from its lowest note (or 1st degree). The eight notes of the scale span an *octave,* which is the closest distance between any two notes with the same name (12 half steps). The 8th degree is an *octave* (twelve half steps) above the 1st degree and has the same note name. Study the placement of whole and half steps represented by the letters "W" and "H" in the following diagram of the C Major scale.

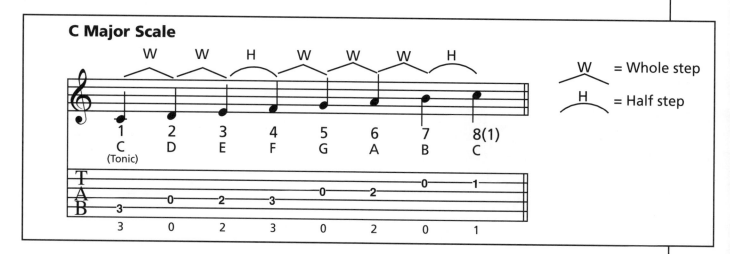

💡 Introducing Triads

A chord is three or more notes played at the same time. In this section, we'll look at chords with three notes, which are called *triads,* and chords with four notes, such as *7th* chords.

There are four qualities of triads: *major, minor, diminished* and *augmented.* We'll look at each triad in two ways: as built from intervals and as derived from the major scale. Choose whichever is easier for you.

Major triads are formed by choosing a root note, then adding a major 3rd and a perfect 5th above it. You can also build a major triad by choosing the root, 3rd and 5th scale degrees of any major scale. Here is how we build a C Major chord:

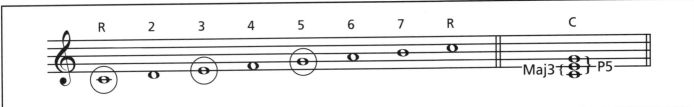

Minor triads are formed by choosing a root note, then adding a minor 3rd and a perfect 5th above it. You can also build a minor triad (abbreviated "min") by choosing the root, lowered 3rd (♭3) and 5th of any major scale. Here is the C Minor chord:

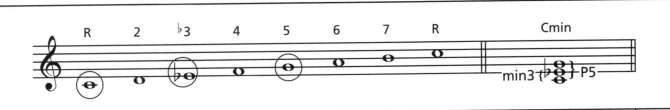

Diminished triads are formed by choosing a root note, then adding a minor 3rd and a diminished 5th above it. You can also build a diminished triad (abbreviated "dim") by using the root, lowered 3rd (♭3) and lowered 5th (♭5) of any major scale. The symbol ○ is often used to indicate a diminished triad. Here is the C Diminished chord:

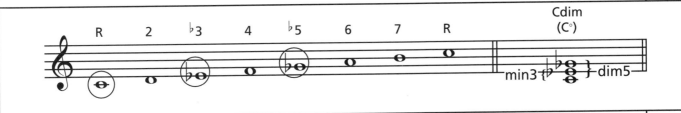

Augmented triads are formed by choosing a root note, then adding a major 3rd and an augmented 5th above it. You can also build an augmented triad (abbreviated "aug") by using the root, 3rd and augmented 5th (♯5) of any major scale. Here is the C Augmented chord:

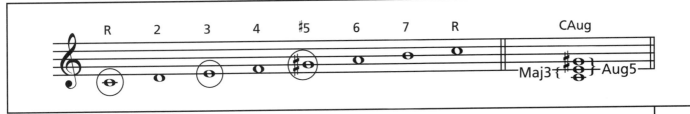

💡 Four-Note Chord Preview

Triads can be extended to become four-note chords. You will learn about the most common of these, *7th chords*, in which some form of the 7th scale degree is added to a triad, beginning on page 20. Of course, other scale degrees besides the 7th can be used in chords. Other types of chords involve adding the 9th scale degree (the 9th is the same note name as the 2nd scale degree), the 11th (the same name as the 4th) and the 13th (the same name as the 6th). When a chord is named 9, 11 or 13, it is understood that the 7th scale degree is present in the chord as well. If the 7th degree is not present, the chord is designated as an *added 9* (add9) or 11 or 13. So, a C9 chord must contain a B♭ in addition to a D, whereas a Cadd9 needs only the D added to the C Major triad.

💡 Major Chord Scales

Diatonic triads are the triads that result from building a triad on every note of a scale, *using only notes from that scale.* Each key has seven diatonic triads. This set of seven triads is called a *chord scale.* Knowing what chords are diatonic to a given key is an essential skill. Saying that a chord is "in the key of C" is identical to saying that a chord is "diatonic to the key of C."

Here's a fool-proof method for generating the diatonic triads of any major key:

1. Begin with the seven notes of the given key's major scale.
2. Add a 3rd and a 5th above each scale degree by stacking 3rds above the notes. This creates a triad for each scale step. Each 3rd and 5th must be a member of that major scale.
3. The resulting order of chord qualities is:
    major, minor, minor, major, major, minor, diminished.

Let's generate the diatonic chords of C Major with the method described above. Start with the seven notes of the C Major scale:

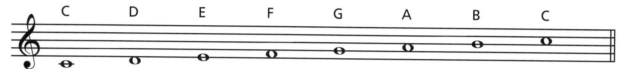

Then, add a 3rd and a 5th above each scale tone. Only notes from the C Major scale are used. For instance, the triad built on C is spelled C, E, G because E is the diatonic 3rd above C, and G is the diatonic 5th above C. Finally, we check the order of chord qualities. Notice the Roman numeral above each chord. Uppercase Roman numerals are used to indicate major or augmented triads. Lowercase Roman numerals are used to indicate minor or diminished triads.

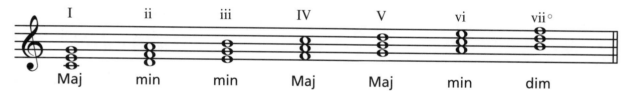

Here's a summary of the diatonic triads of any major scale:

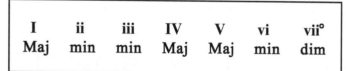

I	ii	iii	IV	V	vi	vii°
Maj	min	min	Maj	Maj	min	dim

Maj = Major
min = Minor
dim = Diminished

💡 Chord Progressions

The common *chord progressions* (sequences of chords) we hear in popular musical styles like rock, folk and blues are usually diatonic chords. Below is an example of playing chords from the C Major chord scale to make a progression. The I chord , vi chord, ii chord and V chord in the key of C are C, Amin, Dmin and G, respectively. Play through the chords from left to right.

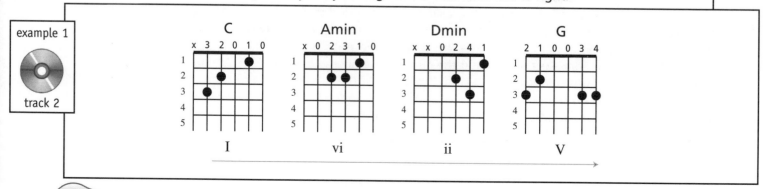

example 1

track 2

💡))) **Chord Idea Book** — Review the Basics

Try playing these chords on your guitar: G, Amin, Bmin, C, D, Emin and F#dim. Listen to the bass notes. You will hear them outline the major scale. You have just played the *chord family* (the chord scale) in the key of G with *open chords* (chords with open strings). Knowledge of chord families and their basic progressions is essential to anyone who wants to become a better musician.

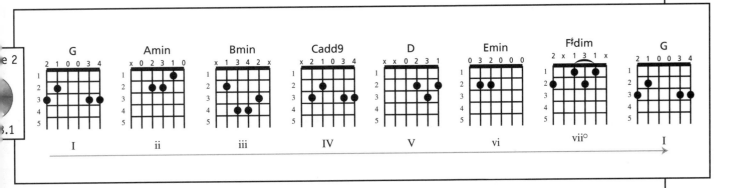

The chart on the right shows the most commonly used open position chord families. Notice that the I chords are the CAGED chords introduced on page 5. The first row shows the C family, the second shows the A family, and so on. All of the chord embellishment lessons in this book will be based on this chart, so make sure you learn it!

I	ii	iii	IV	V	vi	vii°
C	Dmin	Emin	F	G	Amin	Bdim
A	Bmin	C#min	D	E	F#min	G#dim
G	Amin	Bmin	C	D	Emin	F#dim
E	F#min	G#min	A	B	C#min	D#dim
D	Emin	F#min	G	A	Bmin	C#dim

💡 Minor Chord Scales

If the song you are playing or writing is in a minor key, you would use the *natural minor* chord scale. It is known as the natural minor because the notes are the same as in the major scale, only starting on a different scale degree. When the notes of the major scale are played beginning and ending on the 6th scale degree, you have the *relative minor* scale. The 6th degree is a minor 3rd (three frets) down from the tonic of the major scale. (For example, the relative minor of C Major is A Minor). Play the chord scale starting from this note, using only the notes of the natural minor scale.

i	ii°	III	iv	v	VI	VII
Amin	Bdim	C	Dmin	Emin	F	G
Emin	F#dim	G	Amin	Bmin	C	D

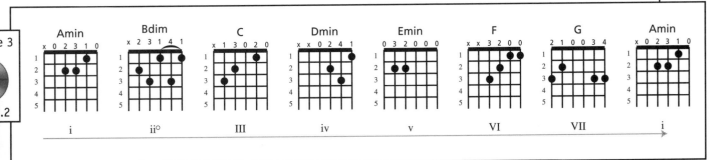

chapter 1 Fingerpicks and strums

💡 Fingerpicking Patterns

Fingerpicking is most effective in an intimate musical setting, such as when the guitar is the sole accompaniment for a singer or when you are playing in a very small ensemble. Fingerpicking allows the guitarist to play bass notes along with melody notes, which makes for a full sound very suitable for accompaniment.

In fingerpicking technique, the fingers of the right hand are referred to by the letters *p*, *i*, *m* and *a*. These letters come from the the classical guitar tradition which uses the Spanish names for the fingers (*p*ulgar = thumb, *i*ndice = index, *m*edio = middle, *a*nular = ring). Most often, *p* plays the bass strings (4, 5 and 6), *i* plays the 3rd string, *m* plays the 2nd and *a* plays the 1st.

Below are five important patterns everyone should know. Notice the *ties* ⌣ in the music. The second note in a tie is not struck. Rather, the first note is held for the combined duration of the tied notes.

Notice the use of *two-voice stemming*. Since the guitar is capable of playing more than one part simultaneously (for example, bass and melody), some notes will have stems going upward and others will have stems going downward to show which part they belong to. Still others will have two stems to show that they function in both parts.

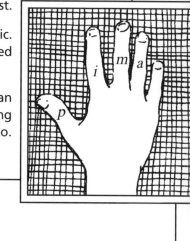

example 4

track 4

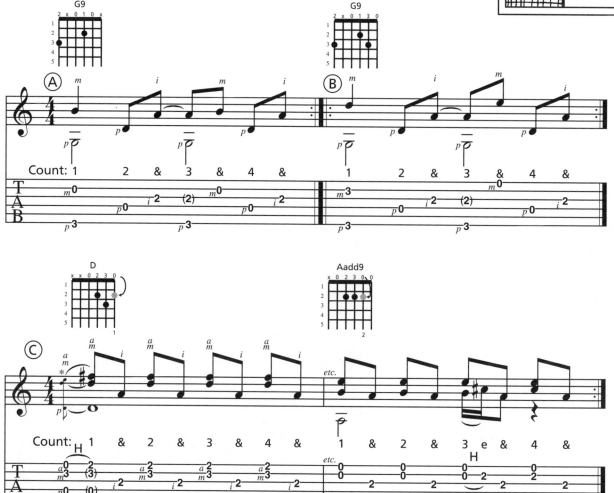

*This is a *grace note*, a quick ornamental note played just before the main note. In this case, the grace note is played on the beat.

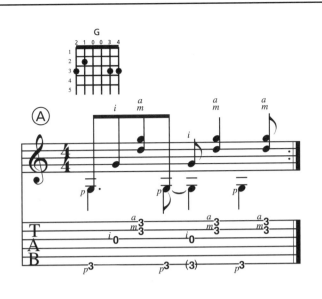

A

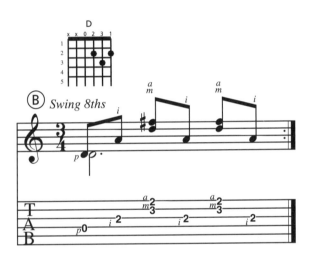

B *Swing 8ths*

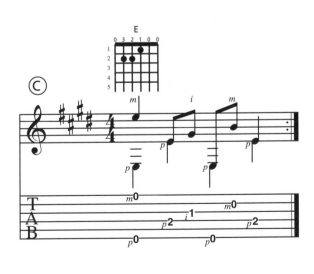

C

Dotted Notes
A dot to the right of a note indicates that the note's value is increased by half.

♩. = Dotted quarter note (1½ beats)

♩. = Dotted half note (3 beats)

Swing 8ths
This term refers to a style of playing eighth notes in which they are played unevenly, in an inexact way. The first note in each pair of eighth notes is played long, causing the second eighth to be delayed and shortened. This is a common "feel" in blues and jazz. See page 18 for more about swing 8ths.

Travis Picking

Below are two examples of *Travis picking*. Travis picking is named for the fingerpicking style of the legendary country guitarist Merle Travis. It is characterized by steady quarter notes in the bass (played with *p*), often alternating between the root and 5th (or sometimes the 3rd) of the chord. This is called an *alternating bass*. The other three fingers (*i*, *m* and *a*) play eighth notes in syncopation with the thumb.

The chart below lists a number of patterns which you can apply to the chords of your choice. Read any line of the chart below from left to right and you will know which string to pick next. The music in Example 6 shows how the shaded patterns would be executed. Be sure to become proficient at reading and understanding these patterns, as they are useful to have in your repertoire, especially as accompaniments (also, charts like this are a cool way to write down your ideas quickly and easily).

Practice Techniques:
- Practice with a metronome. This will help you play evenly and with consistancy.
- The two strings on beat one are struck together. Master this first.
- Then try omitting the "&" of 4 (the last eighth note in the measure, in the "optional" column in the chart). This is a common variation.
- Play the pattern as written.

(52) = These notes can b[e] plucked togethe[r]

Here are two examples to show how the patterns read and apply.

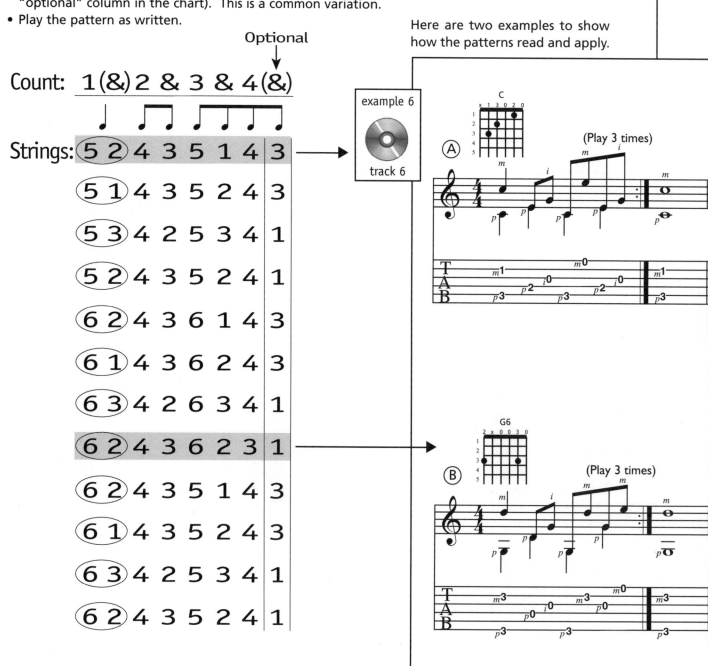

Count: 1 & 2 & 3 &
Strings: 5 3 2 1 2 3

5 1 2 3 2 1

5 3 2 3 1 3

5 3 2 3 1 2

5 1 2 1 3 2

5 1 2 1 3 1

5 2 3 2 1 2

5 2 1 2 1 3

5 3 1 2 1 2

5 3 1 2 3 2

5 2 3 1 2 3

5 1 3 2 1 2

5 1 3 2 3 2

Notice that example 7A is in ¾ which has only three beats in the measure.

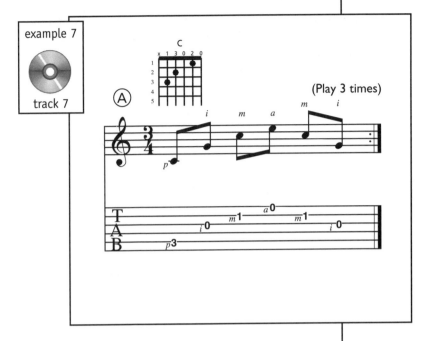

Count: 1 & 2 & 3 & 4 &
Strings: 5 3 2 3 1 3 2 3

5 3 1 3 2 3 1 3

5 1 2 3 1 2 3 2

5 3 2 1 2 3 1 2

5 1 3 2 1 2 3 2

5 1 3 2 1 3 2 3

5 3 2 1 2 3 2 1

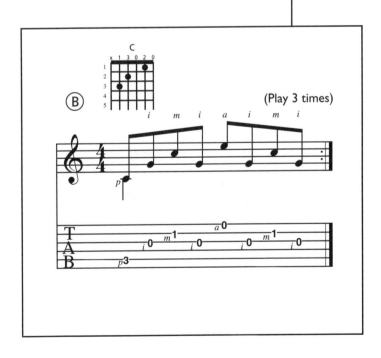

 ## Strumming Patterns

The guitar can be thought of as a percussion instrument with strings. The guitar part is often vital to the rhythm of a piece. Your right hand is your time keeper. Here are some strumming patterns that are useful to know and that work well in a variety of styles.

These examples are written in *rhythmic notation*, which does not represent actual pitches but tells you when and how to strum. The note values are the same as in standard notation. When a notehead is represented in standard notation rather than a slash (as in example 8 C and D), play that note as written.

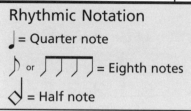

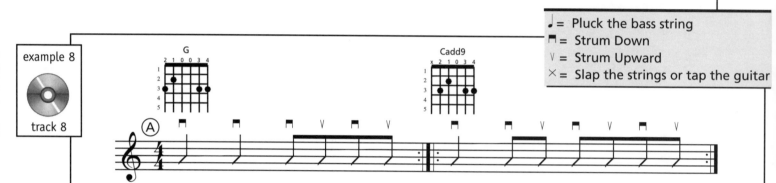

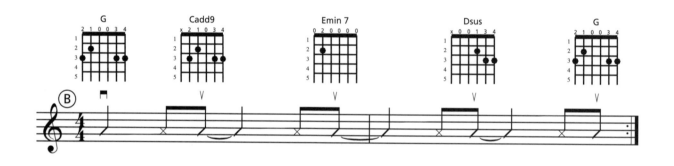

Notice the alternating bass in (D).

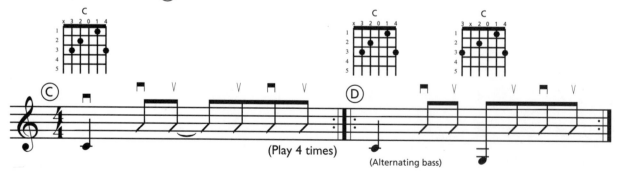

(Play 4 times)   (Alternating bass)

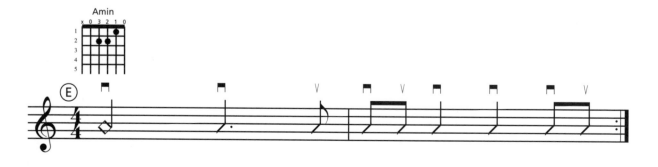

C = *Cut time*. The half note gets one beat, the quarter note gets one half beat, the eighth note gets one quarter beat, etc.

C/G = A *slash chord*. The first letter is the chord name and the second letter is the bass note.

Count: 1 & 2 & 1 & 2 & 1 & 2 ee ah 1 & 2 ee ah

Count: 1 & 2 & 1 & 2 & 1 & 2 & 1 & 2 &

* (1x) = Play these chords the first time through. (2x) = Play these chords the second time through.

Blues and Steady Bass Rhythm

The following rhythm ideas have a typical blues feel. The bass notes are steady and give the music its drive, while the chords and licks "dress it up." This is fundamental in solo blues playing. Apply these rhythms to a twelve-bar blues pattern. Once you're comfortable with the exercises, play them while muting the bass notes with your right palm. Watch how this gives the music that thumpin' feel!

Swing 8ths

These exercises introduce the concept of *swing feel*. In swing feel, the eighth notes are not played evenly, but in the feel of an eighth note *triplet* with the first two notes tied together. A triplet is three notes in the time of two.

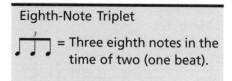

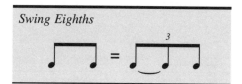

Remember that swing feel is indicated in music by the term *swing 8ths*. When you see this, you know that you are to play the eighth notes unevenly, even though they look even.

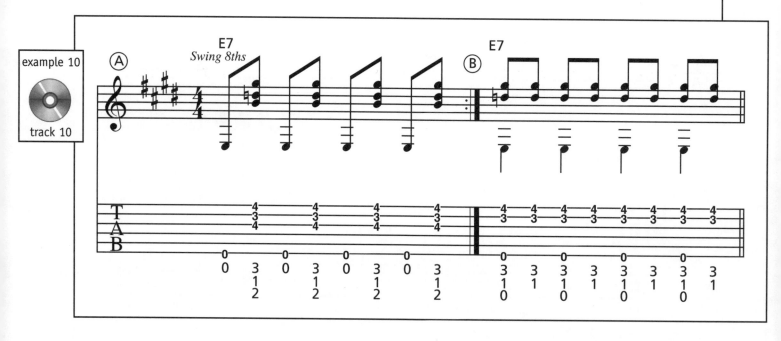

Bends and Grace Notes

The next two examples involve the technique of *bending*. The number over the arrow tells you how far to bend the string. In this case, you bend it a half step.

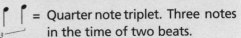

½ = Bend the 2nd string so that it sounds one half step higher.

= Quarter note triplet. Three notes in the time of two beats.

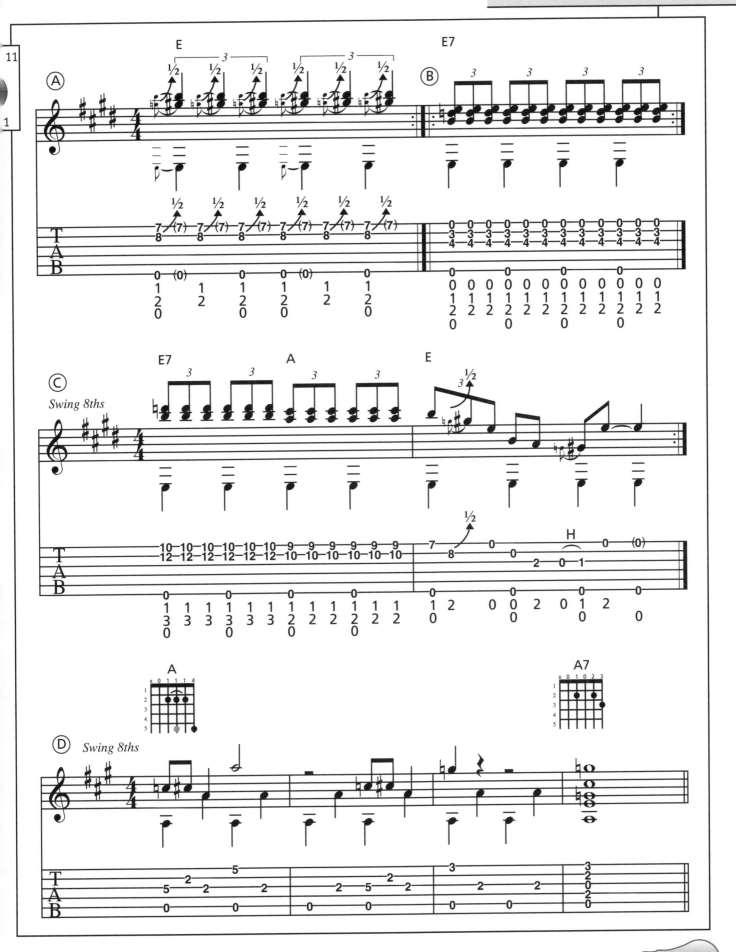

💡 Four-Note Chords

There are many types of four-note chords, the most common of which are *7th chords*. A 7th chord is created by adding an additional 3rd above a triad to create a four-note chord. The added note is a 7th above the root of the chord. There are four kinds of 7th chords: major 7th (Maj7), minor 7th (min7), dominant 7th (7) and minor 7th flat five (min7♭5, sometimes referred to as half-diminished 7th, or ∅7). Another important four-note chord, the *diminished 7th* (dim7 or °7), is discussed on page 26.

As we did with the triads, we'll build each 7th chord with intervals and from the major scale. We'll use the key of C Major again.

Major 7th chords are formed by adding a major 3rd to the top of a major triad (a major 7th above the root). So, they consist of the root, 3rd, 5th and 7th scale degrees. Here is a C Major 7th chord (CMaj7):

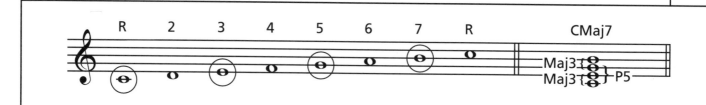

Minor 7th chords are formed by adding a minor 3rd to the top of a minor triad (a minor 7th above the root). They use the root, ♭3, 5th and ♭7 scale degrees. Here is a C Minor 7th chord (Cmin7):

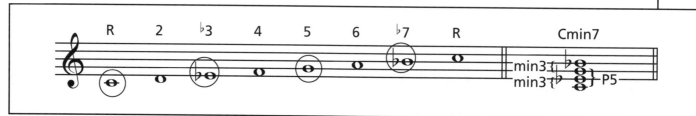

Dominant 7 chords are formed by adding a minor 3rd to the top of a major triad (a minor 7th above the root). They consist of the root, ♭3, 5th and ♭7 scale degrees. Here is a C Dominant 7th chord (C7):

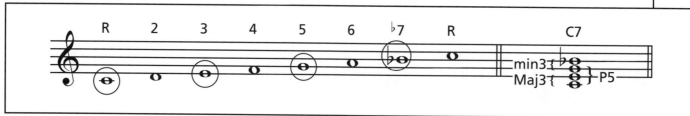

Minor 7♭5 chords are formed by adding a major 3rd to the top of a diminished triad (a minor 7th above the root). They use the root, ♭3, ♭5 and ♭7 scale degrees. Here is a C Minor 7♭5 chord (Cmin7♭5):

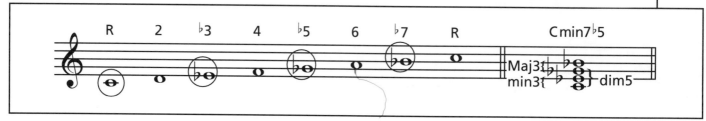

💡 7th-Chord Scales

Diatonic 7th chords are the chords that result from building a 7th chord on every note of a scale, using only notes from that scale. Each key has seven diatonic 7th chords. As with the diatonic triads, knowing what 7th chords are diatonic to a given key is an essential skill.

Here's a fool-proof method for generating the diatonic 7th chords of any major key:

1. Begin with the seven notes of the given key's major scale.
2. Add a 3rd, a 5th and a 7th above each scale degree by stacking 3rds above the notes. This creates a 7th chord for each scale step. Remember that each added tone must be a note from that major scale.
3. The resulting order of chord qualities is:
   Major 7, minor 7, minor 7, Major 7, Dominant 7 (7), minor 7, minor 7 flat 5 (min7$^\flat$5).

Let's generate the diatonic 7th chords of C Major using the method described above. Start with the seven notes of the C Major scale:

Then, add a 3rd, a 5th and a 7th above each scale tone. Only notes from the C Major scale are used. For instance, the 7th chord built on C is spelled C, E, G, B because E is the diatonic 3rd above C, G is the diatonic 5th above C and B is the diatonic 7th above C. Finally, we check the order of chord qualities. Notice the Roman numeral above each chord. Uppercase Roman numerals are used to indicate major or augmented chords. Lowercase Roman numerals are used to indicate minor or diminished chords.

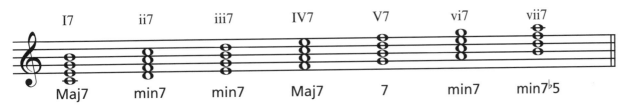

Here's a summary of the diatonic 7th chords of any major scale:

I7	ii7	iii7	IV7	V7	vi7	vii7
Maj7	min7	min7	Maj7	Maj7	min7	min7$^\flat$5

> Maj = Major
> min = Minor
> dim = Diminished

💡 Chord Progressions

The common *chord progressions* (sequences of chords) we hear in popular musical styles like rock, folk and blues often involve diatonic 7th chords. Below is an example using 7th chords from the C Major chord scale to make a progression. The I chord, vi chord, ii chord and V chord in the key of C are CMaj7, Amin7, Dmin7 and G7, respectively. Play through the chords from left to right.

chapter 2

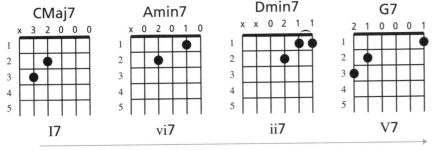

The chord diagrams in chapters 2 through 6 are variations of basic chords that you already know. They can all be used to spice up or embellish the basic shapes. Many are based on the original chord shapes and have the same roots, so they are easy to apply in place of the original chord. Don't be put off by some of the new chord names, such as min7, add9 or sus4. They are simply "souped-up" versions of the original chords.

We will be learning the chord embellishments of each basic chord in the context of that chord's function in a given chord family (page 11). The chord families we will cover are those for the keys of C, A, G, E and D. If a chord appears in more than one family (and most of them do), you will have different options because chords have different functions in different keys. For example, if the G chord or its embellished version is functioning as a V (*dominant*) chord, you will see that it "behaves" differently from the way it functions as a I (*tonic*) chord.

Useful tip:

Because of string spacing and/or the nature of the chord's sound, some chords sound better fingerpicked than they do strummed, and vice-versa. It is always a good idea to have a pencil in your guitar case so that you can make notes to yourself when you learn about details such as this.

C is the first chord in our CAGED formula. Let's check out its family.

The chord family in the key of C is:

C	Dmin	Emin	F	G	Amin	Bdim(or Bmin7♭5)
I	ii	iii	IV	V	vi	vii°

Here are some embellishments for each chord in the C family.

Reminders:

○ = Optional note
● = Add note
(= Hammer-on

💡 C Ideas — The I chord

example 12

track 12

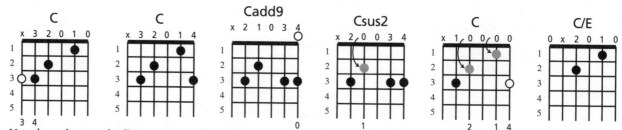

Numbers beneath diagrams are for optional and added notes, or indicate an alternate fingering.

C Ideas — The I chord (continued)

Csus4   **C**   **C to Csus**   **Cadd9**   **CMaj7**   **C/E**

The *unisons* (two identical notes) ringing together give the chords on the right a droning sound much like a mountain dulcimer.

Cadd9   **C**

Dmin Ideas — The ii chord

Dmin   **Dmin7(11)**   **Dsus4**   **Dmin7**   **Dmin7**

Dmin/F   **Dmin7**   **Dmin7**   **Dmin7**   **Dmin7/A**

D5   **Dmin11**   **Dmin**   **Dmin**   **Dmin7/F**

💡 Emin Ideas — The iii chord

example 18

track 14.1

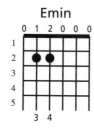

example 19

track 14.2

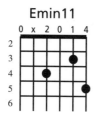 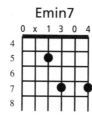 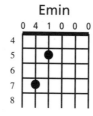 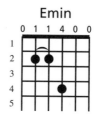 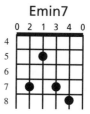

💡 F Ideas — The IV chord

T = Left Thumb

example 20

track 14.3

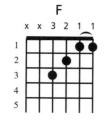 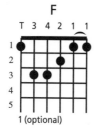 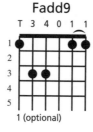 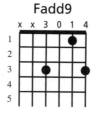 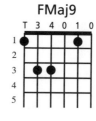 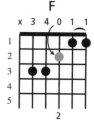

example 21

track 14.4

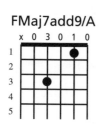 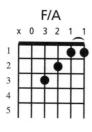 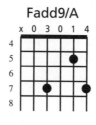 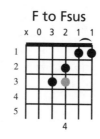

💡 **Chord Idea Book** — Chapter 2

💡 G Ideas — The V chord

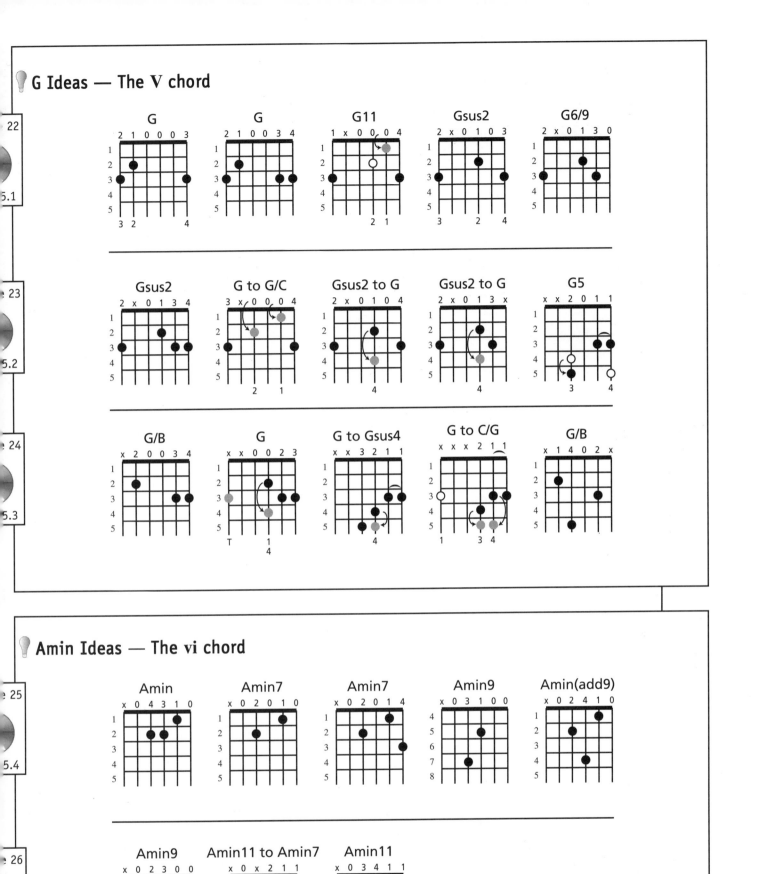

💡 Amin Ideas — The vi chord

The diminished 7 and min7♭5 chords appear in many different styles. Here are the easiest ways to play them.

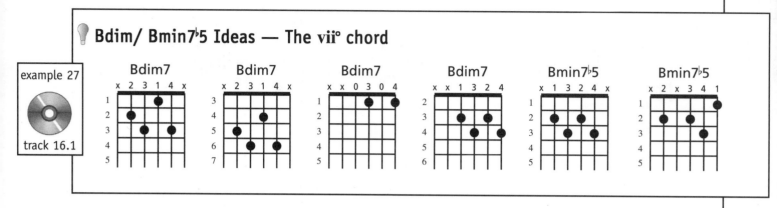

💡 Bdim/ Bmin7♭5 Ideas — The vii° chord

example 27
track 16.1

Bdim7   Bdim7   Bdim7   Bdim7   Bmin7♭5   Bmin7♭5

Note: There are only three different *diminished 7* (dim7) chords. A dim7 chord is constructed by stacking three minor 3rds. If you build a diminished 7 chord starting on C, you will get the notes C, E♭, G♭ and A (technically B♭♭)*. Move up a half step and you have C♯, E, G and B♭. Go up one more half step and the notes are D, F, A♭ and B (technically C♭). The diminished 7 chord starting on E♭ contains the same notes as the chord starting on C, and the pattern thus continues. These are moveable chord forms, so you can move the same shape up or down a minor 3rd (three frets) and you'll always be playing the same diminished 7 chord.

Cdim7

💡 Common Chord Progressions

Try using these new chord embellishments.

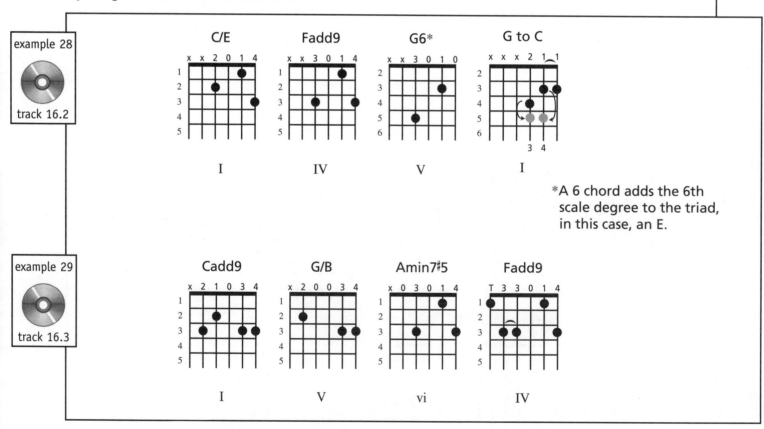

example 28
track 16.2

C/E   Fadd9   G6*   G to C

I   IV   V   I

*A 6 chord adds the 6th scale degree to the triad, in this case, an E.

example 29
track 16.3

Cadd9   G/B   Amin7♯5   Fadd9

I   V   vi   IV

* Some notes have two different letter names. These are called *enharmonic equivalents*. An enharmonic note is a note that sounds the same and is played at the same fret as another note like F♯ and G♭. The note is referred to as a sharp if the natural note is raised by a half step and it's referred to as a flat if the natural note is lowered by a half step.

Here are some more chord progressions for you to try. Use the embellishments you have learned.

C	G	F	C		C	Amin	Dmin	G
I	V	IV	I		I	vi	ii	V
C	Dmin	Amin	G		C	F	Dmin	G
I	ii	vi	V		I	IV	ii	V
C	Emin	F	G		C	Amin	G	F
I	iii	IV	V		I	vi	V	IV

💡 Common "Ear Twisters"

Below are some common but perhaps unexpected chord changes that will "surprise" the ear in the key of C. Notice that some of the chords are clearly not in the key of C. Sometimes beautiful results are achieved by using *non-diatonic* chords such as these.

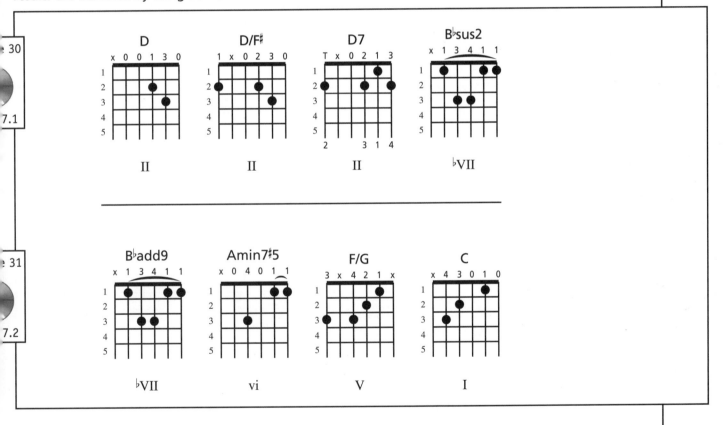

Sus4 and sus2 chords

Sus (short for *suspended*) chords are very common in guitar playing. They are major triads whose 3rd is replaced by either a 4th above the root (sus4) or a major 2nd above the root (sus2). So, a Gsus4 would consist of G, C and D — the C replaces the 3rd (B) that would normally be in the chord. A Csus2 contains C, D and G with the D replacing the 3rd (E). In some cases, the suspension, whether the 4th or 2nd, moves to the 3rd, giving a feeling of completion to the music. This is called a *resolution*. Suspensions can also be built on minor triads, and 7, 9, 11 and 13 chords can contain suspensions as well.

💡 An Etude for the C Family

By the Sea is an *etude* (a piece written for the development of a particular technique) written to put some of the new chords we've studied into a musical context. The chord diagrams will show you the chord shapes and fingerings as the tune moves along. In your fingerpicking, try to let the notes sustain and ring against each other. Practice this etude in small sections and take it slowly. Always keep in mind the relationship of the embellished chord you are playing to the original chord shape from which it came. You can then apply each bit of musical information you learn to your own accompaniments or compositions.

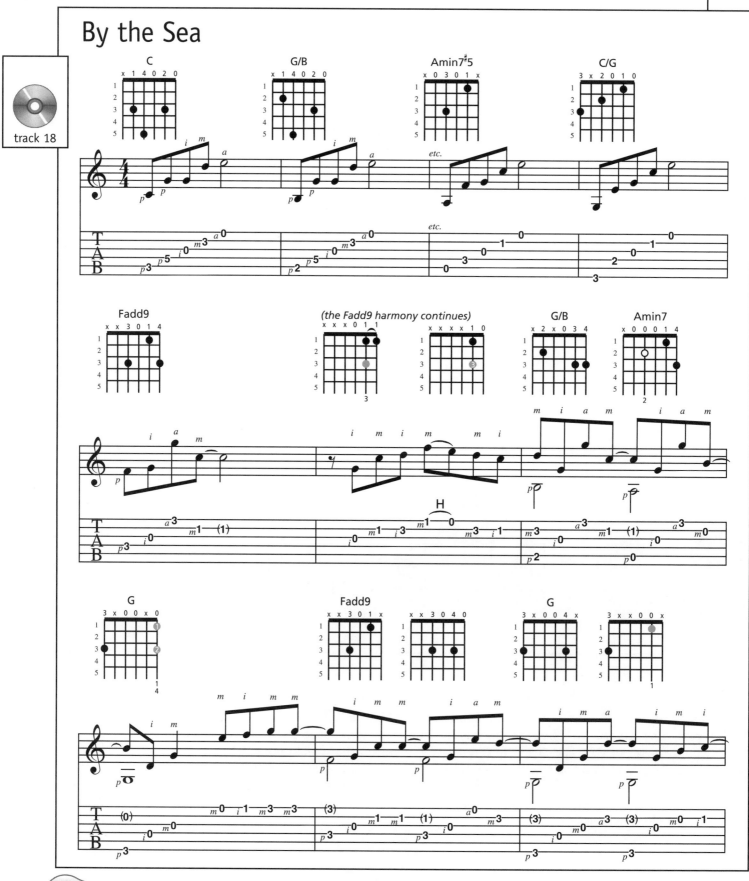

By the Sea

track 18

💡 **Chord Idea Book** — Chapter 2

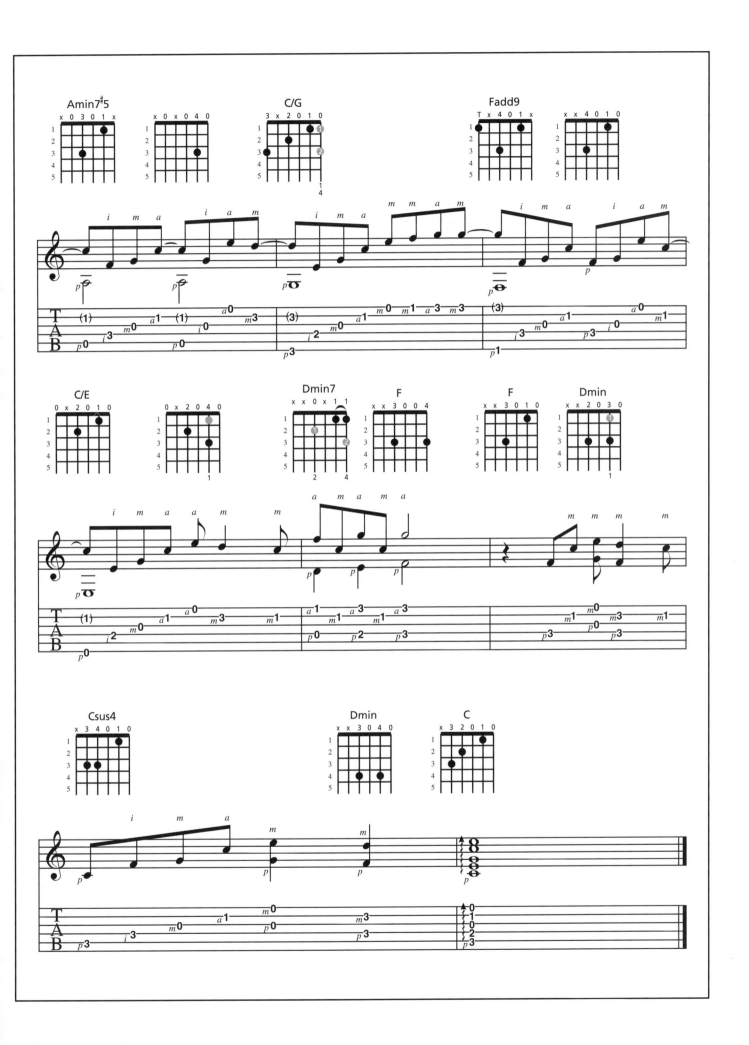

A is the next chord in the CAGED formula. Let's take a look at the chord family for A Major.

The chord family in the key of A is:

A	Bmin	C#min	D	E	F#min	G#dim (or G#min7♭5)
I	ii	iii	IV	V	vi	vii°

Here are some embellishments for each chord in the A family.

💡 A Ideas — The I chord

 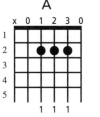

 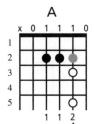

The following chords have the root on the high E string. These are good ending chords for songs in the key of A:

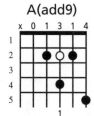 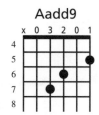

💡 Bmin Ideas — The ii chord

💡 C♯min Ideas — The iii chord

36

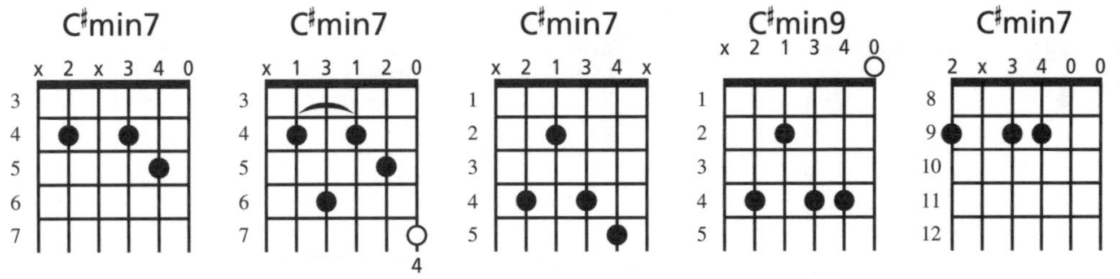

0.1

C♯min7	C♯min7	C♯min7	C♯min9	C♯min7

💡 D Ideas — The IV chord

37

0.2

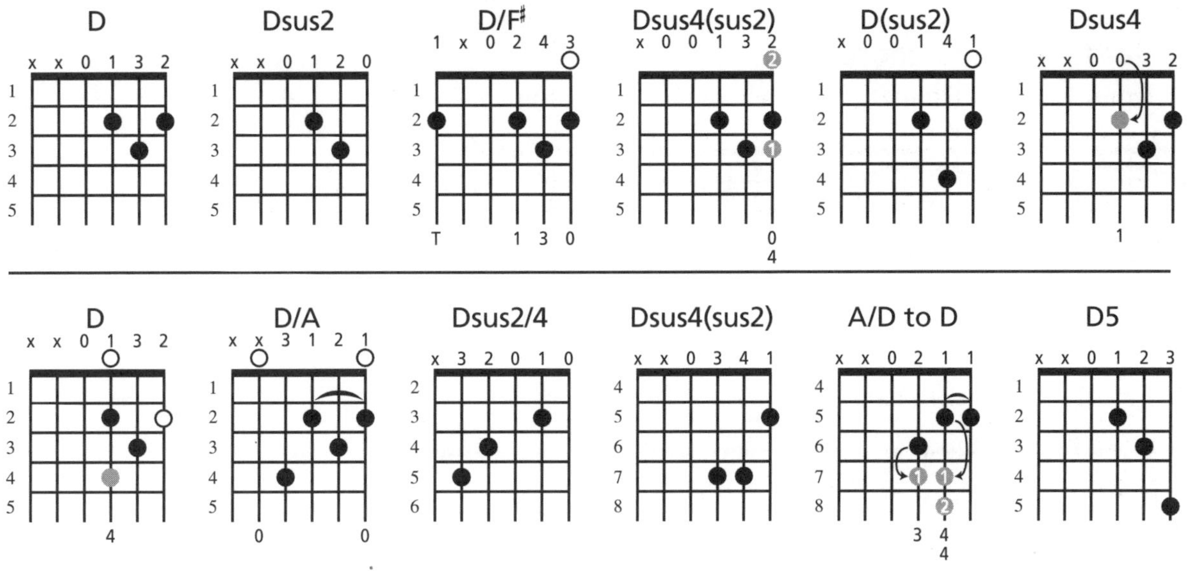

D	Dsus2	D/F♯	Dsus4(sus2)	D(sus2)	Dsus4

38

0.3

D	D/A	Dsus2/4	Dsus4(sus2)	A/D to D	D5

💡 E Ideas — The V chord

39

0.4

Eadd9	Esus4 to E	E5	D/E	D/E

40

0.5

E	E/G♯	D/E	E13sus4	Esus4

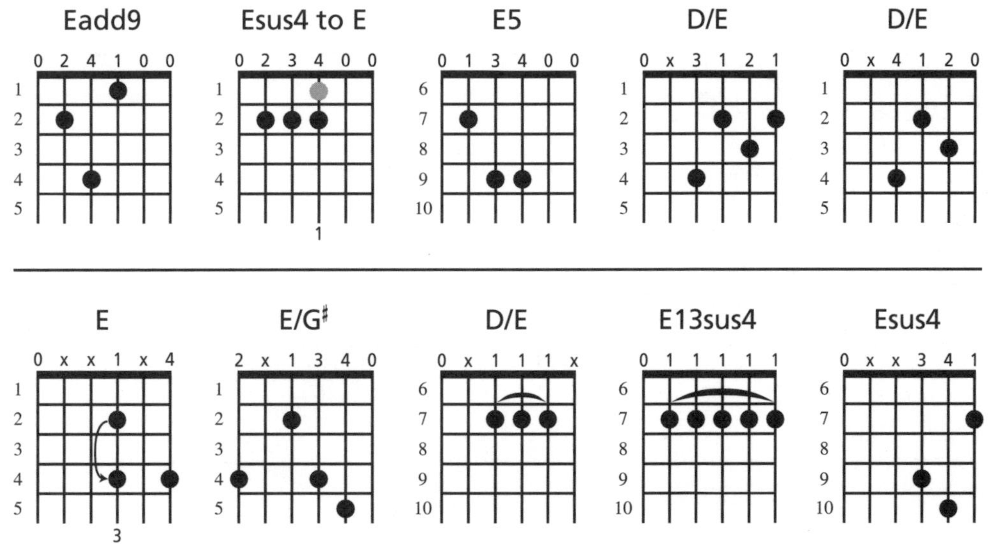

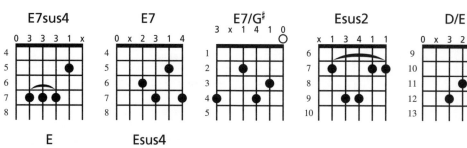

E7sus4   E7   E7/G#   Esus2   D/E

E   Esus4

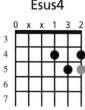

F#min Ideas — The vi chord

F#min   F#min7   F#min11   *F#min11/C#

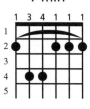

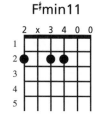
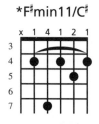

*This one sounds lush if another instument plays F# as the root.

F#min7   F#min7   F#min11   F#min11

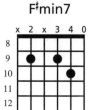

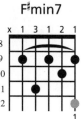
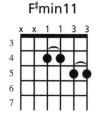
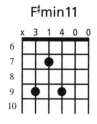

Here are some of the diminished and min7♭5 chords of the A family. (See page 26 for a brief discussion of diminished 7 chords).

G#dim/G#min7♭5 Ideas — The vii° chord

G#dim   G#dim   G#min7♭5   G#min7♭5   G#min7♭5

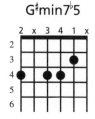
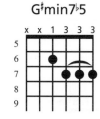
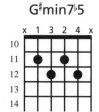

💡 Common Chord Progressions

Try applying some new chord embellishments to some simple chord progressions. Here is an example:

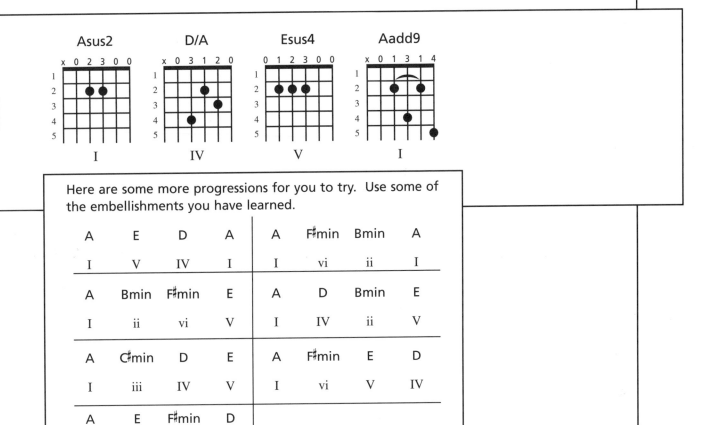

Here are some more progressions for you to try. Use some of the embellishments you have learned.

A	E	D	A		A	F♯min	Bmin	A
I	V	IV	I		I	vi	ii	I
A	Bmin	F♯min	E		A	D	Bmin	E
I	ii	vi	V		I	IV	ii	V
A	C♯min	D	E		A	F♯min	E	D
I	iii	IV	V		I	vi	V	IV
A	E	F♯min	D					
I	V	vi	IV					

💡 Common "Ear Twisters"

Here are some of the unexpected chords of the A family. These could work well in the bridge section or interlude of a song.

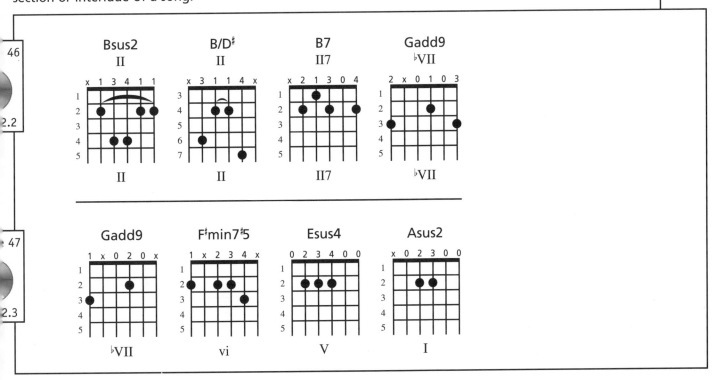

Etude for the A Family

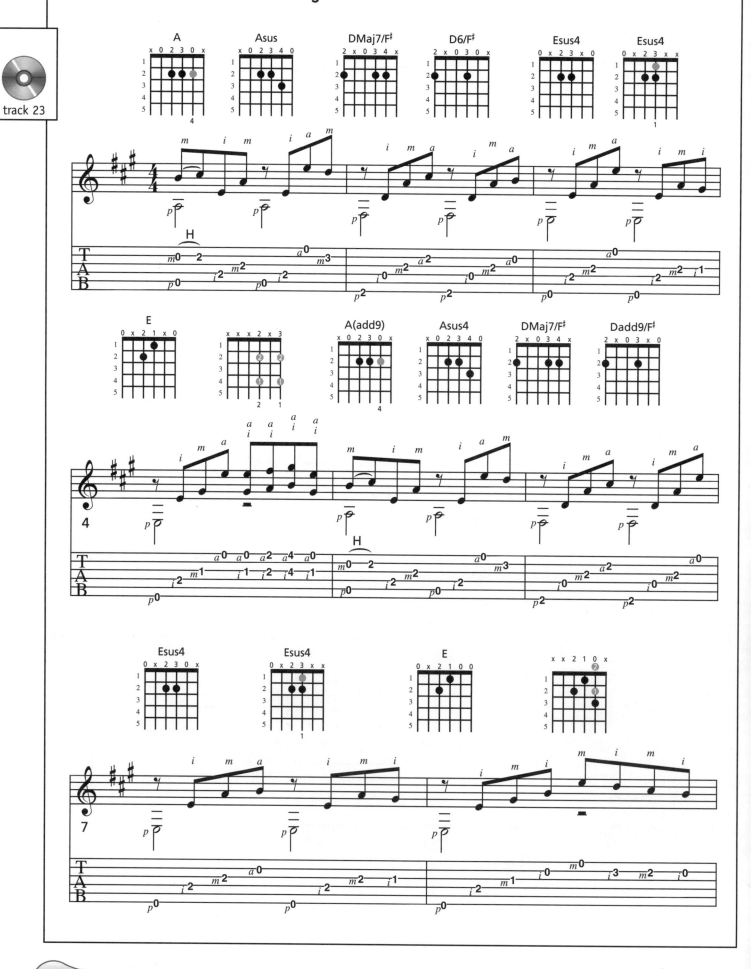

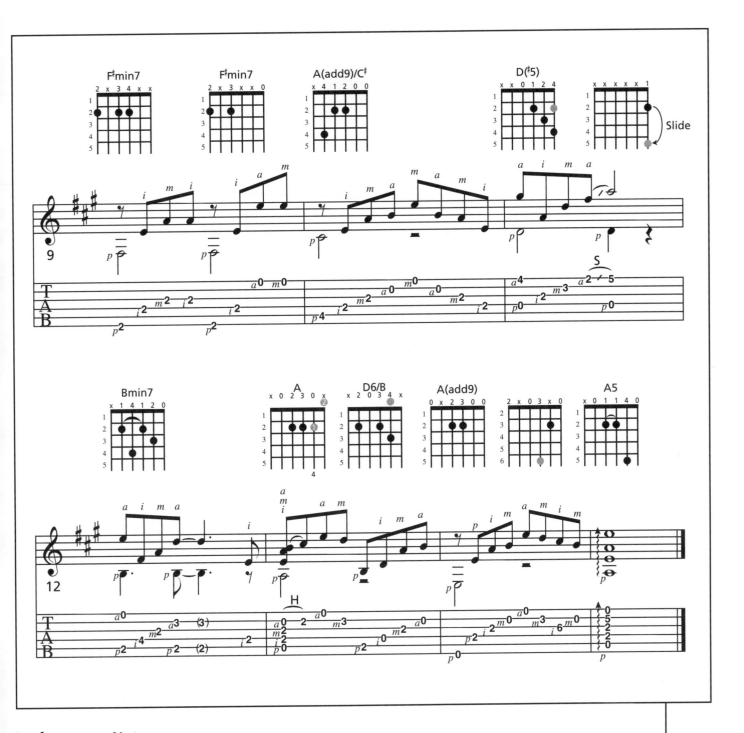

Performance Notes

Etude for the A Family uses many of the chord embellishments that we looked at in this chapter. Let the notes sustain as if you were using the sustain pedal on a piano. Slightly slow the *tempo* (speed) on the last two beats of bar 4 (this is called *rit.* or *ritardando*, which is the Italian word meaning to slow down). At bar 5, return to your original speed (the Italian for this technique is *a tempo*, which literally means "back to the time"). Subtle details like varying your tempo or *dynamics* (volume) will make your music much more interesting. Measures 9-12 are the most challenging of this etude, so practice them slowly until you are comfortable with them. Only when you can play them with ease and confidence should you increase the tempo. Another good practice idea is to play a measure, or even a section of a measure, repeatedly until you are ready to move on. This is called *looping*. Remember, you can and should take the ideas in these etudes and apply them to your own playing. Put your own personality into the music and make the music your own. The composer wrote the notes, but it's the player who interprets those notes and brings the music "to life."

The chord family in the key of G is:

G	Amin	Bmin	C	D	Emin	F#dim or (F#min7♭5)
I	ii	iii	IV	V	vi	vii°

💡 G Ideas — The I chord

example 48

track 24.1

G   **G**   **Gsus4(add9)**   **Gadd9**   **G/B**

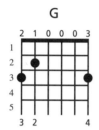
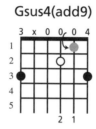
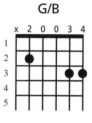

example 49

track 24.2

G6/9   **Gadd9**   **G to C/G**   **GMaj7**   **G/D**

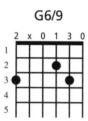
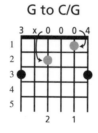
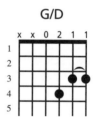

example 50

track 24.3

GMaj7   **Gadd9 to G**   **Gsus2 to G**   **G5**   **GMaj7**

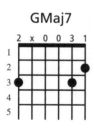
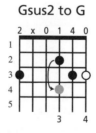
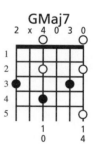

example 51

track 24.4

G(add9)   **G to Gsus4**   **G to C/G**   **GMaj7/B**

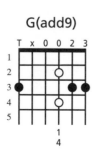
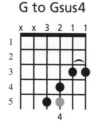
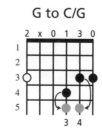
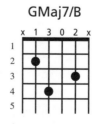

💡 Amin Ideas — The ii chord

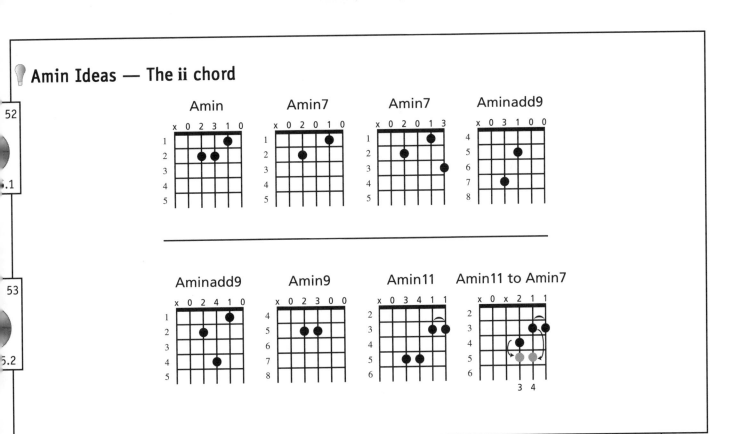

Amin   Amin7   Amin7   Aminadd9

Aminadd9   Amin9   Amin11   Amin11 to Amin7

💡 Bmin Ideas — The iii chord

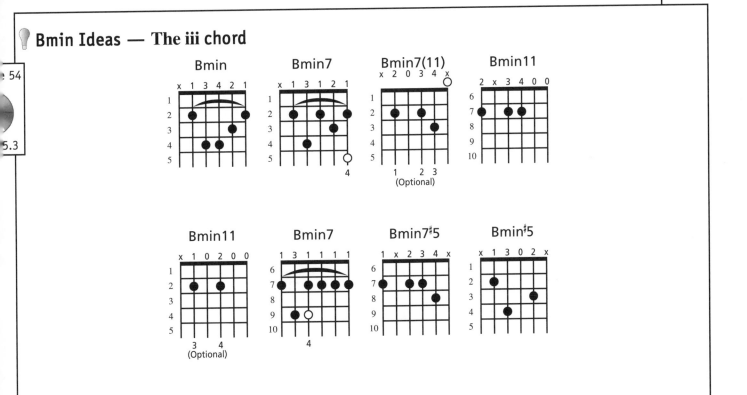

Bmin   Bmin7   Bmin7(11)   Bmin11

Bmin11   Bmin7   Bmin7#5   Bmin#5

💡 C Ideas — The IV chord

Cadd9

Cadd9
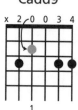

Cadd9#11
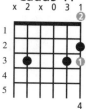

C

Cadd9

Cadd9

C
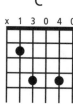

C/E to Csus4
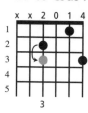

Csus4
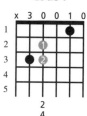

💡 D Ideas — The V chord

, ‾ , = Barre if not using optional note.

Dsus2
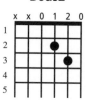

D/F#
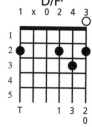

Dsus4 to Dsus2
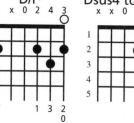

Dadd9
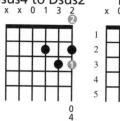

D11
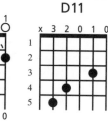

Dsus4/A
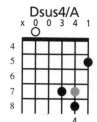

C6/D or D9sus4
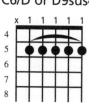

D5
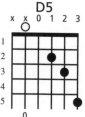

Dsus2
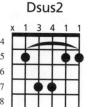

D7/F#
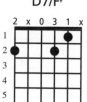

C/D
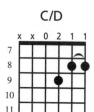

D7sus4

C/D

C/D

D/F#

💡 Emin Ideas — The vi chord

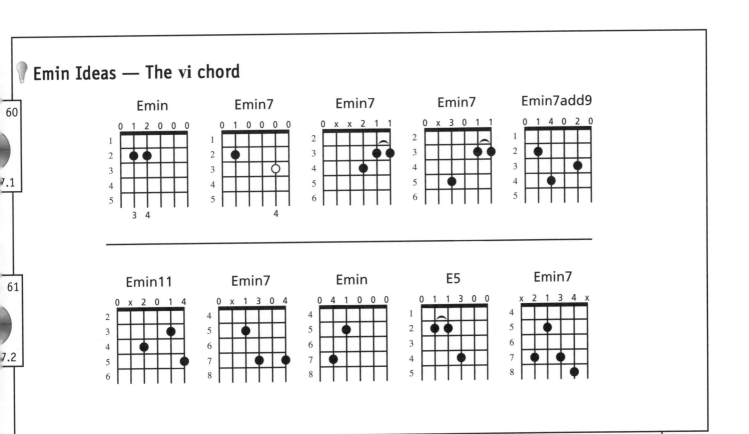

Here are some of the diminished and min7♭5 chords of the G family (see page 26 for a brief discussion of diminished 7 chords).

💡 F♯dim/F♯min7♭5 Ideas — The vii° chord

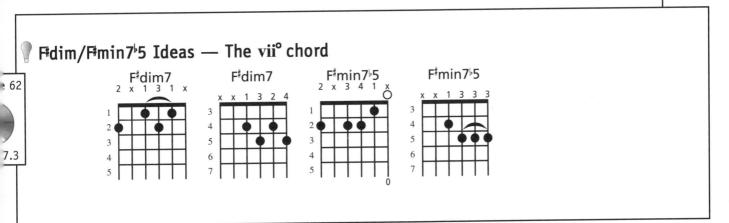

💡 Common Chord Progressions

Apply some new chord embellishments to these simple chord progressions.

example 63

track 28.1

example 64

track 28.2

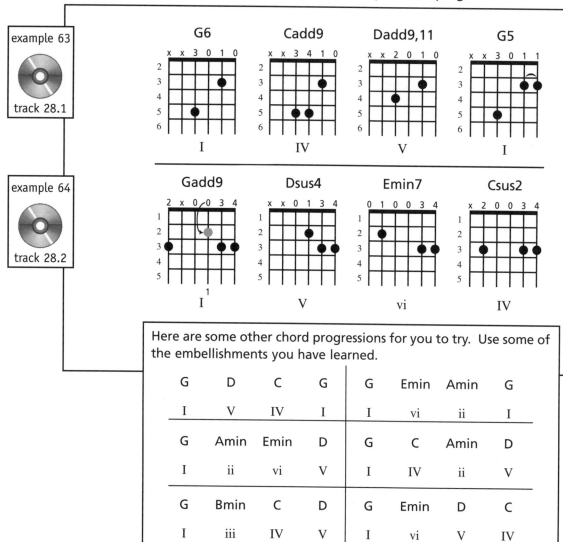

Here are some other chord progressions for you to try. Use some of the embellishments you have learned.

G	D	C	G	G	Emin	Amin	G
I	V	IV	I	I	vi	ii	I

G	Amin	Emin	D	G	C	Amin	D
I	ii	vi	V	I	IV	ii	V

G	Bmin	C	D	G	Emin	D	C
I	iii	IV	V	I	vi	V	IV

💡 Common "Ear Twisters"

Here are some of the unexpected chords of the G family. The use of chords that are not normally associated with a particular key is another way to make your music interesting and fresh.

example 65

track 28.3

example 66

track 28.4

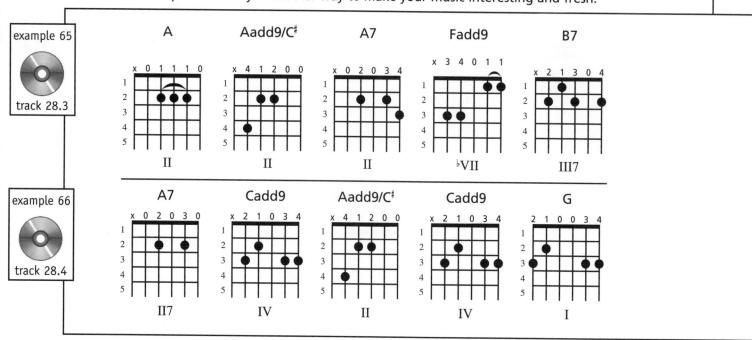

The key of E Minor uses the same chords as for G Major. Enjoy the *Little Etude in E Minor*.

Little Etude in E Minor

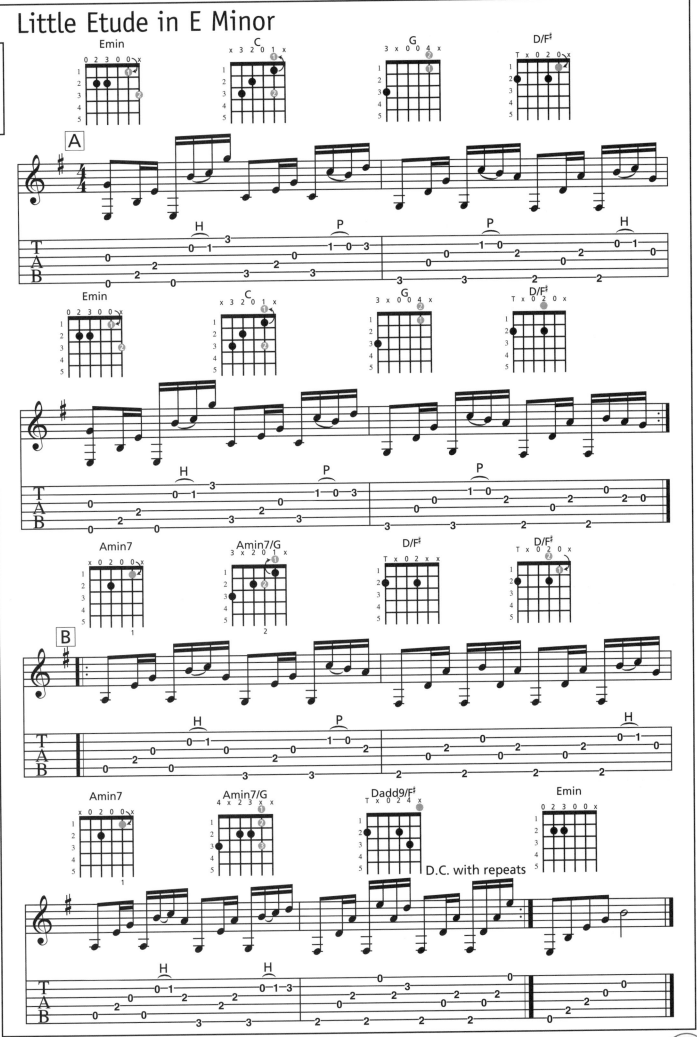

Etude for the G Family

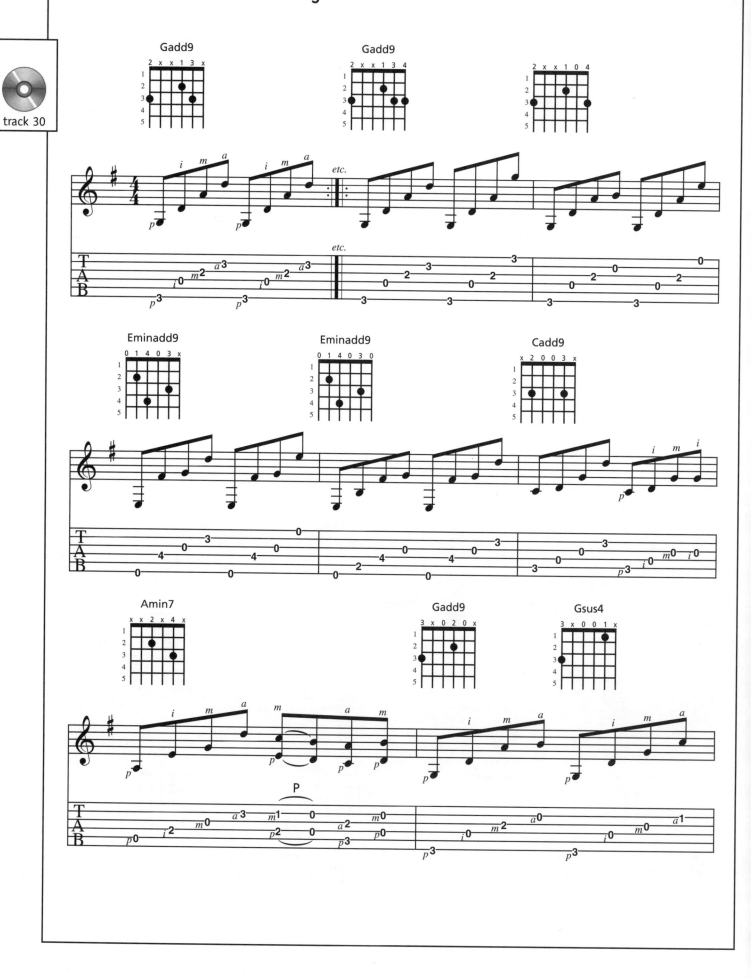

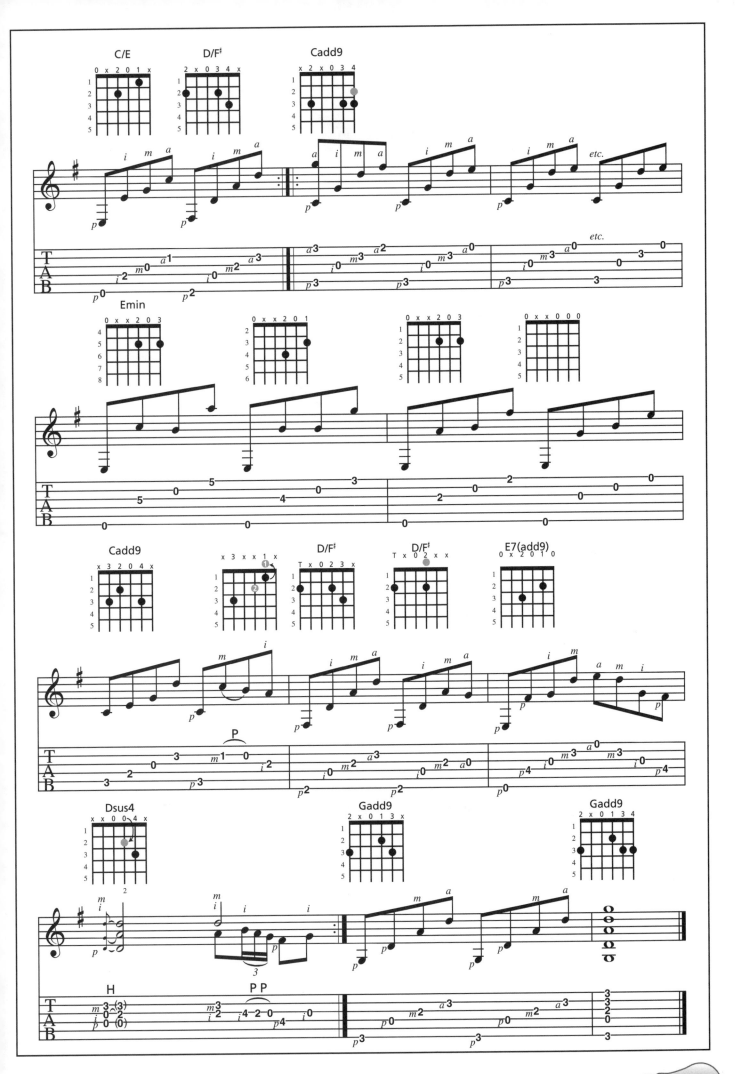

chapter 5

E Major family chord embellishments

The chord family in the key of E is:

E	F#min	G#min	A	B	C#min	D#dim (or D#min7♭5)
I	ii	iii	IV	V	vi	vii°

Here are some embellishments for each chord in the E family.

💡 E Ideas — The I chord

example 67

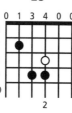
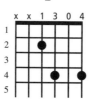
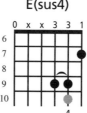
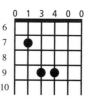

example 68

track 31.2

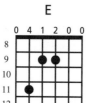
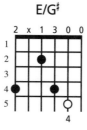
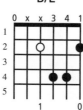
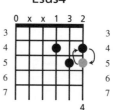
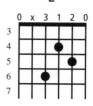

example 69

track 31.3

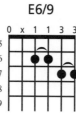
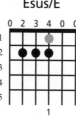
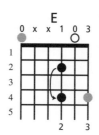
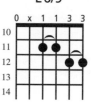

💡 F#min Ideas — The ii chord

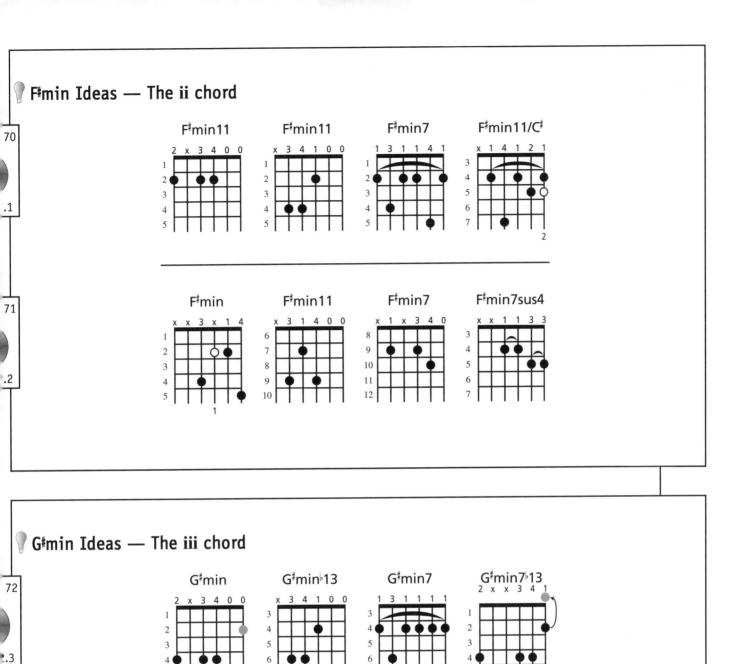

F#min11 F#min11 F#min7 F#min11/C#

F#min F#min11 F#min7 F#min7sus4

💡 G#min Ideas — The iii chord

G#min G#min♭13 G#min7 G#min7♭13

G#min7sus4 G#min G#min7 G#min11/D#

💡 A Ideas — The IV chord

example 74
track 33.1

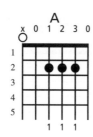 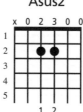 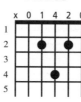 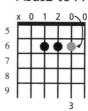

example 75
track 33.2

 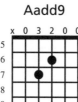 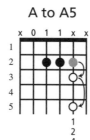 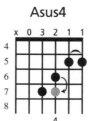 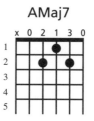

When you're playing in the key of E, it's easy to get caught on the V chord (B). Many players are intimidated by barre chords so they put the capo on and play in a different chord family. Unfortunately, doing this causes you to miss out on the low E. You will probably find that these B voicings sound better and are easier to play than barre chords.

💡 B Ideas — The V chord

example 76
track 33.3

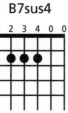  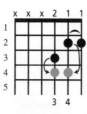  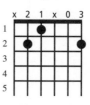 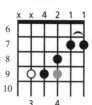

example 77
track 33.4

  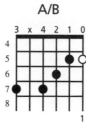 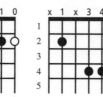 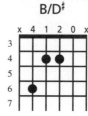

C#min Ideas — The vi chord

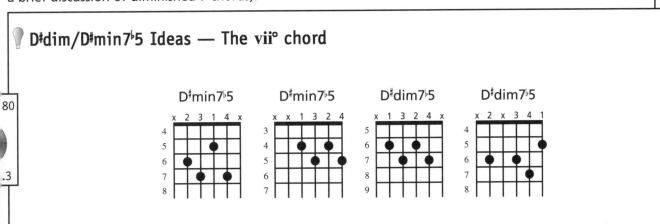

C#min7

C#min7

C#min11 to C#min9

C#min7

C#min7

C#min7

C#min7

C#min11

Here are some easy ways to play the diminished and min7♭5 chords of the E family (see page 26 for a brief discussion of diminished 7 chords).

D#dim/D#min7♭5 Ideas — The vii° chord

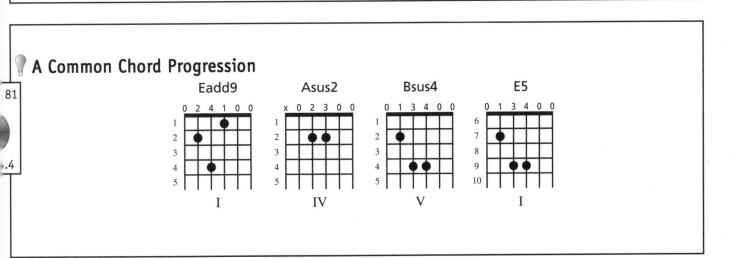

D#min7♭5

D#min7♭5

D#dim7♭5

D#dim7♭5

A Common Chord Progression

Eadd9

Asus2

Bsus4

E5

I

IV

V

I

Eternal Highway (Strumming Etude for the E Family)

Chord Idea Book — Chapter 5

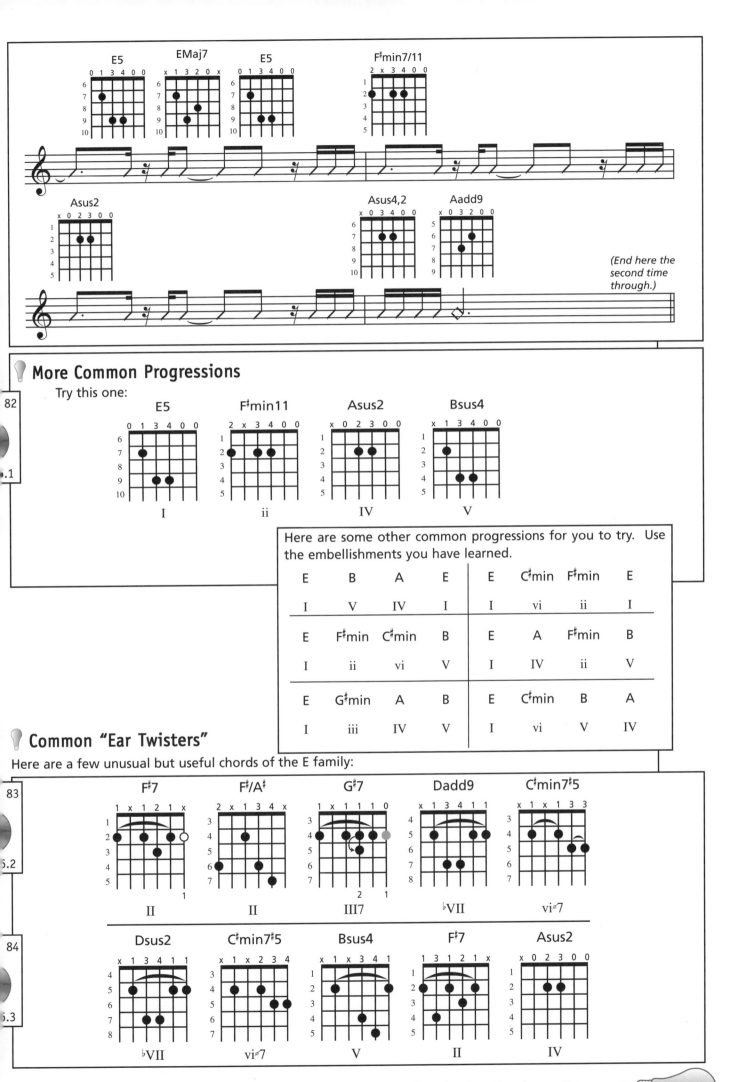

More Common Progressions

Try this one:

E5	F#min11	Asus2	Bsus4
I	ii	IV	V

Here are some other common progressions for you to try. Use the embellishments you have learned.

E	B	A	E		E	C#min	F#min	E
I	V	IV	I		I	vi	ii	I
E	F#min	C#min	B		E	A	F#min	B
I	ii	vi	V		I	IV	ii	V
E	G#min	A	B		E	C#min	B	A
I	iii	IV	V		I	vi	V	IV

Common "Ear Twisters"

Here are a few unusual but useful chords of the E family:

F#7	F#/A#	G#7	Dadd9	C#min7#5
II	II	III7	♭VII	vi∅7

Dsus2	C#min7#5	Bsus4	F#7	Asus2
♭VII	vi∅7	V	II	IV

The chord family in the key of D is:

D	Emin	F#min	G	A	Bmin	C#dim (or C#min7♭5)
I	ii	iii	IV	V	vi	vii°

Here are some embellishments for each chord in the **D** family:

💡 D Ideas — The I chord

example 85

track 37.1

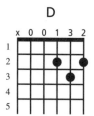

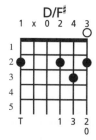

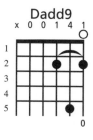

example 86

track 37.2

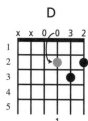

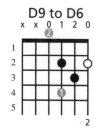

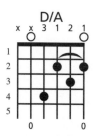

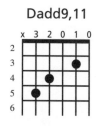

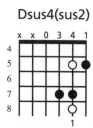

example 87

track 37.3

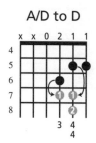

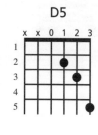

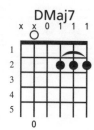

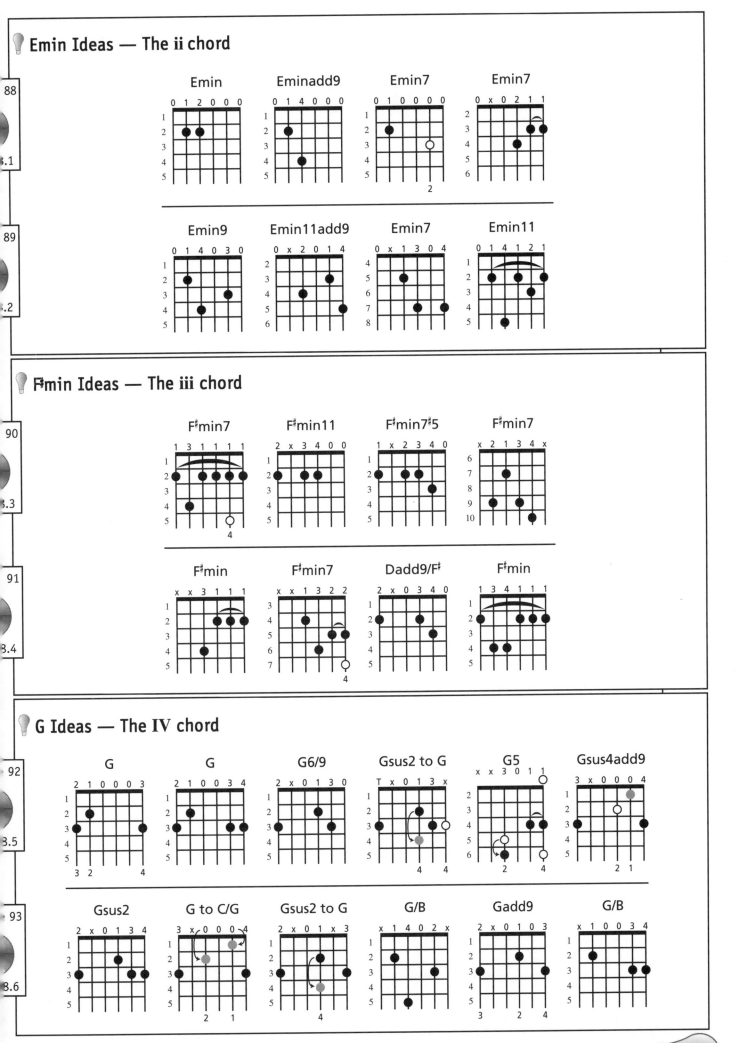

Emin Ideas — The ii chord

F#min Ideas — The iii chord

G Ideas — The IV chord

💡 A Ideas — The V chord

A7sus4   Asus2   G/A   Asus4   G/A

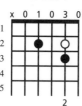

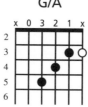
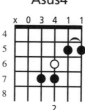

A7(13)   A5   Asus4   Aadd9/C♯   Aadd9

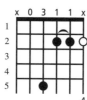
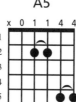

Aadd9sus4 to Aadd9   Dsus4 to A   A to D/A   Aadd9

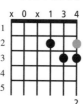
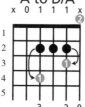
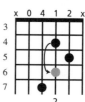

💡 Bmin Ideas — The vi chord

Bmin11   Bmin11   Bmin11   Bmin7

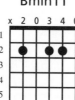

Bmin7   B5   Bmin11   Bmin11

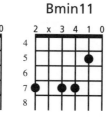

Here are the easiest ways to play the diminished and min7♭5 chords of the D family (see page 26 for a brief discussion of diminished 7 chords).

💡 C♯dim/C♯min7♭5 Ideas — The vii° chord

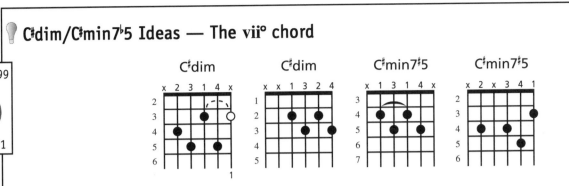

💡 Common Chord Progressions

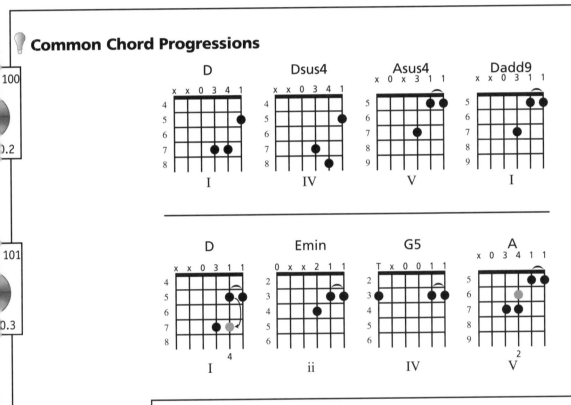

Here are some other common chord progressions for you to try. Use the embellishments you have learned.

D	A	G	D		D	Bmin	Emin	A
I	V	IV	I		I	vi	ii	V
D	Emin	Bmin	A		D	G	Emin	A
I	ii	vi	V		I	IV	ii	V
D	F♯min	G	A		D	Bmin	A	G
I	iii	IV	V		I	vi	V	IV

💡 Common "Ear Twisters"

Here are some of the less common but very effective chords of the D family:

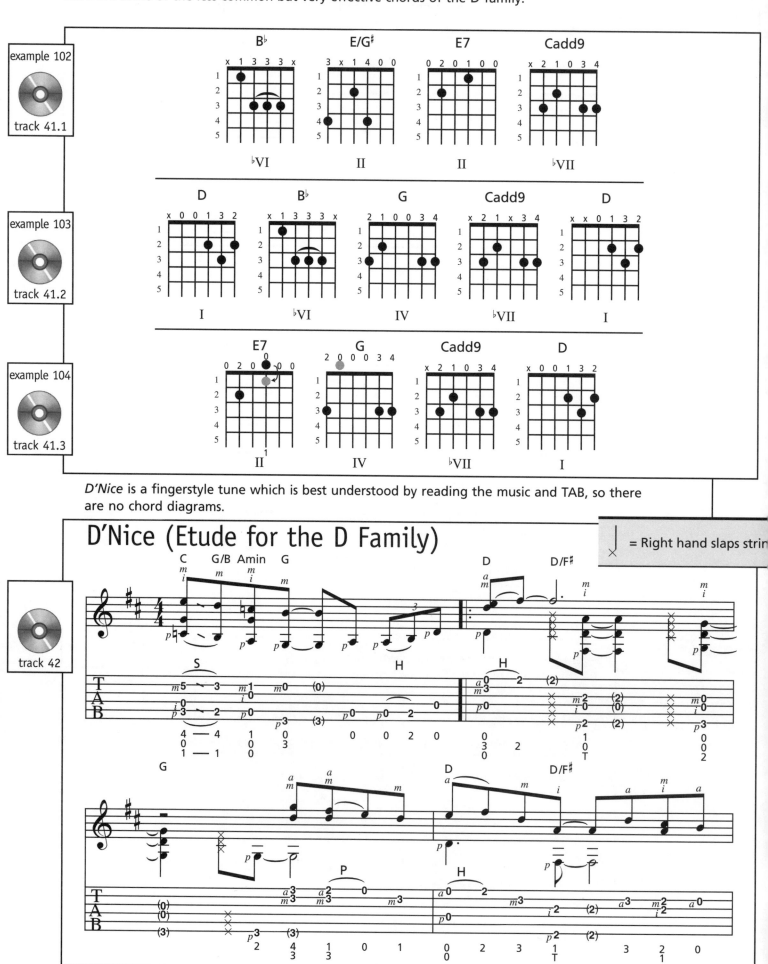

D'Nice is a fingerstyle tune which is best understood by reading the music and TAB, so there are no chord diagrams.

D'Nice (Etude for the D Family)

= Right hand slaps strin[g]

chapter 7 capos are cool!

Capos are both a blessing and a necessity. They make for easy and good-sounding *transpositions* (key changes), and they are also an excellent tool for creating beautiful and colorful chord sounds. Here is what's great about a capo:

It will allow you to transpose to different keys without having to change chord shapes.

A capo shortens the vibrating length of the guitar strings, thus raising their pitch. For example, when the capo is attached to the 2nd fret, the 2nd fret acts like a new *nut* (the resting place for the strings below the 1st fret). In this case, the 2nd fret notes are now the open strings. The 6th string has been transposed up a whole step from E to F♯, the 5th string from A to B, etc. So, when a C chord form is played, it sounds like D! When a G chord form is played, it sounds like A, etc.

Reasons to Transpose

There are ordinarily two reasons to change the key of a piece of music. The first is that many times a song is too low or too high for a singer, so by transposing the song into his or her vocal range, the singer may perform the song with a minimum of difficulty. The second is that different keys have different characteristics. For example, a certain key might have a bright sound, while another key might sound more subdued. This is often the reason that a composer chooses to put a song into a particular key.

Here is a list of reasons to use a capo:

If you need to change the key of a song for a singer.

If you want to give new character to an instrumental piece.

If you have to play in an unfamiliar key and you only know the basic chords.

If you want to have more *inversion* (a chord played with something other than the root in the bass) options for a specific key, but you still want the open string "ring" that the original open chord form gives you. See "Capos in action" below.

If you are looking for a wider range of sound when two or more guitars are playing. When a band has more than one guitarist, they will sometimes fatten up their sound by playing with their capos in different positions.

Capos in Action

Using a capo allows you to play familiar chord shapes in different keys and to create a higher inversion of the original chord. You will often find that the "capoed" version of a chord sounds better for a particular song, and that the chord progression lies more easily under the fingers when certain chords come around. In the example below, the capo is clamped to the 2nd fret and, when a C chord shape is played, a D chord results.

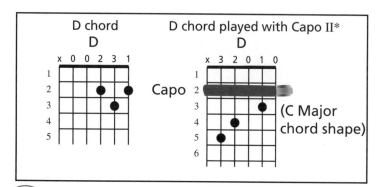

As you can see, when you use a capo to play the D chord by playing a C shape chord, the result is a different inversion of the chord. In this case, the F♯ is now in the bass.

*When you see Capo II or Capo2, clamp the capo on the 2nd fret.

In order for you to transpose quickly using a capo, it is essential that you know all the notes on the guitar neck! Don't be intimidated by this task! Below is an easy way to get started.

Begin by learning the notes on the 5th and 6th strings, which are the two lowest strings of the guitar. Start by memorizing the natural notes first. Natural notes are those that are neither sharped nor flatted.

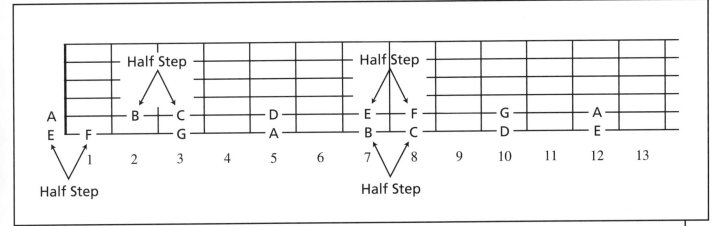

Notice the natural half steps between B and C and E and F. They are only one fret apart. To practice: Choose a natural note (A, B, C, D, E, F or G) and then find it on both the E and A strings. Now that you have learned the natural notes, you can fill in the sharps and flats.

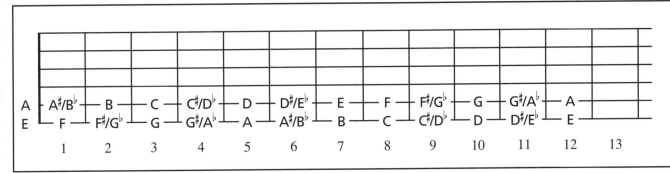

💡 How to Use a Capo to Play in Difficult Keys

This is why you need to know the notes on the neck. Some keys, such as B♭, are more difficult for guitarists to play in than others because they allow for very few, if any, open strings. Find the lowest B♭ on the guitar (the first fret on the 5th string). Place the capo on the 1st fret and play the basic A Major chord shape. The capo has allowed you to use a basic chord shape (A) to play a tricky chord (B♭)! Now, with the capo in place, you can play progressions in the key of A but it will sound like B♭.

Using a capo makes B♭ an easy key

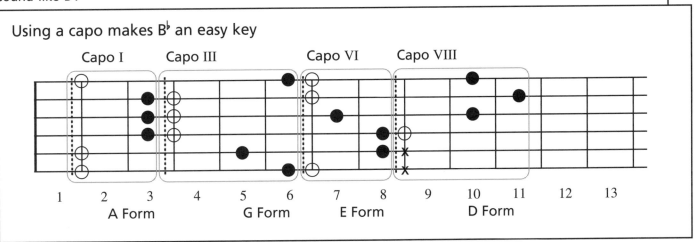

💡 The CAGED Formula

The CAGED chords introduced on page 5 together make a formula that is a good way to find capo positions quickly. Some players who don't know all the notes on the fretboard still know how to find capo positions for different keys by using the CAGED formula. The word CAGED refers to the order in which chord shapes are laid out on the neck. This formula is useful because the C, A, G, E and D chord shapes are familiar to all guitarists, and therefore it is easy to apply the system and learn chord inversions.

The diagram below shows a typical application of the CAGED formula to the C chord. The goal is to find the different positions on the fretboard where simple chord forms can be used to play in the key of C.

Start with the open C Major chord. It is a simple matter to know where to place the capo because in the CAGED formula, you always place it on the highest fret of the previous chord in the formula. Place the capo on the 3rd fret and play an A Major chord. The highest fret in the A form is the 5th fret. So place the capo on the 5th fret and play a G Major chord. Continue this pattern with the E and D shapes. You have now played a C Major chord in five positions, ascending on the fretboard. It's easy! No matter which letter you start with, you'll always go in the order of CAGED. So, the A shape will always come after the C shape, the G shape will follow the A shape, etc.

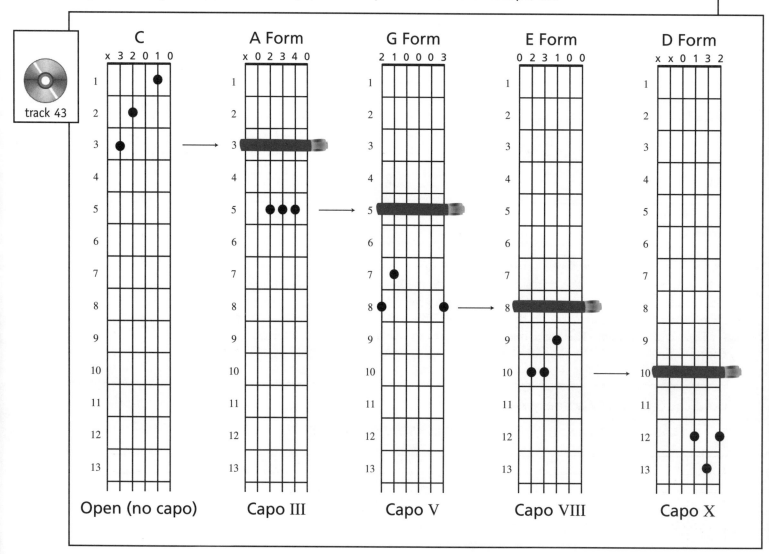

Capo Table

This table shows the different capo positions moving up the fretboard for each key. The CAGED formula is applied to all twelve keys so that you can see a variety of capo positions for the less common keys. Remember, the pattern of chord shapes always goes in the order of CAGED, no matter what shape you start with. So, if the initial shape is A, as in the keys of A, A♯/B♭ and B, the next shape will be the G shape. If the initial shape is D, as in the keys of D and D♯/E♭, repeat back to the beginning of the CAGED formula and the next shape will be C.

Key	Open or 1st Capo Position	2nd Capo Position	3rd Capo Position	4th Capo Position
A	Open / A	Capo II / G	Capo V / E	Capo VII / D
A♯/B♭	Capo I / A	Capo III / G	Capo VI / E	Capo VIII / D
B	Capo II / A	Capo IV / G	Capo VII / E	Capo IX / D
C	Open / C	Capo III / A	Capo V / G	Capo VIII / E
C♯/D♭	Capo I / C	Capo IV / A	Capo VI / G	Capo IX / E
D	Open / D	Capo II / C	Capo V / A	Capo VII / G
D♯/E♭	Capo I / D	Capo III / C	Capo VI / A	Capo VIII / G
E	Open / E	Capo II / D	Capo IV / C	Capo VII / A
F	Capo I / E	Capo III / D	Capo V / C	Capo VIII / A
F♯/G♭	Capo II / E	Capo IV / D	Capo VI / C	Capo IX / A
G	Open / G	Capo III / E	Capo V / D	Capo VII / C
G♯/A♭	Capo I / G	Capo IV / E	Capo VI / D	Capo VIII / C

💡 Different Types of Capos

Many players, such as James Taylor, Jackson Brown, Joni Mitchell and David Wilcox, use modified capos. There are many different types of modified capos available. A few of the better known models are the Kyser capo (with a cut-out for the low E string), the Shubb partial capo (which covers the 3rd, 4th and 5th strings, and is also known as a sus4 capo) and the Kyser banjo capo (which covers 4 strings).

There are quite a few advantages to partial capos. You can get the effect of an *alternate tuning* (see page 71) while staying in standard tuning. A partial capo on the 2nd fret will give you an unfretted *suspended* chord (a chord with an added tone, usually a 2nd or 4th above the root, see page 27) similar to DADGAD tuning (page 78), but transposed to E-B-E-A-B-E.

Here is an example using two capos simultaneously. A normal capo (covering all 6 strings) is at the 2nd fret and a partial capo (covering the 3rd, 4th and 5th strings) is two frets above the normal capo. The cool thing here, as mentioned above, is that you get the effect of an alternate tuning similar to DADGAD while staying in standard tuning.

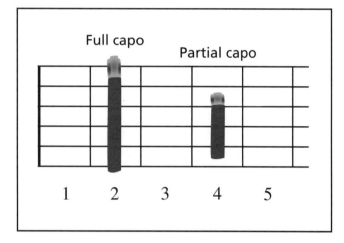

The resulting "open tuning" of this capo combination is F#-C#-F#-B-C#-F#, which is DADGAD transposed up a major 3rd (two whole steps).

Experimenting with capos is a lot of fun. Let your imagination go wild and let your ears and fingers go into new and exciting places. It's a good idea to keep a notebook and tape recorder handy, because you will definitely come across new chord shapes and new tonal colors that you will want to remember. There are endless possibilities on the guitar, with or without a capo. One of the greatest joys of music is that if you keep trying new things, you'll never stop learning new things.

Other guitarists who use capos include Martin Simpson, Willy Porter, Vince Gill, Peter Himillman, Brian Adams, Bonnie Raitt and Eric Clapton.

The nature of the next piece, *Waterfall*, does not lend itself well to chord diagrams. The TAB will help you know exactly where to place your fingers. Have fun!

Waterfall (Etude for Partial Capo)

Partial capo II on strings 3, 4 and 5

💡 Hammer-ons and Pull-offs

One of the most effective ways to embellish an open chord is to sweeten it with a hammer-on or pull-off or both. For example, in his instrumental sections, James Taylor will often play a little hammer-on or pull-off lick and then go back to his normal fingerpicking style when the vocals come back in. You can hear hammer-ons and pull-offs in many different guitar styles, both electric and acoustic. Here are a some cool hammer-on and pull-off ideas within open chords:

FP = Fingerpicked

example 105

track 45

Etude for Hammer-ons and Pull-offs

💡 Passing Tones and Chords

While playing chord progressions, guitatists often play single notes or quick chords between the main chords. These notes help to connect the two chords, they are usually diatonic (of the scale) and they're called *passing tones*. Here are some examples of passing tones used in open chords. The resulting chords are in parentheses. Notice the bass/strum ststyle.

example 107

track 48

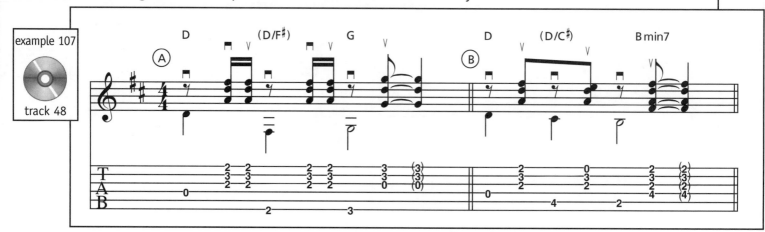

64 💡 **Chord Idea Book** — *Chapter 8*

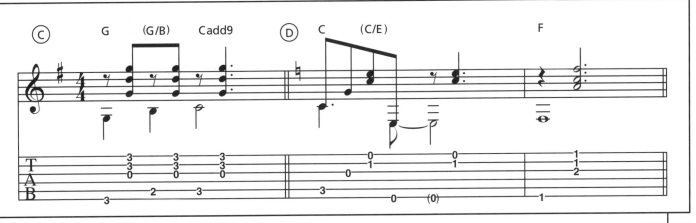

Here are some more passing-chord and passing-tone examples for you to try. You can use the picking style demonstrated in examples 1-4, or create your own. Again, the passing chords are in parenthesis. Have fun.

Ⓐ C — C/E — Fsus2

Ⓑ Cadd9 — G/A — G

Ⓒ Bmin7 — A — G

Ⓓ G — F♯ — Emin

Ⓔ Cadd9 — G/B — Amin7

Ⓕ A — A/C♯ — D

Ⓖ D — D/F♯ — G

Ⓗ E — G♯ — Aadd9

Ⓘ Asus2 — G♯ — F♯min11

Ⓙ Emin — B — Asus2

Ⓚ D — G/B — Cadd9

💡 Pivot Finger Chord Combinations

Here are some examples of chord combinations that share a common finger. When this happens, the stationary finger is called the *pivot finger*. This is nice because it allows for as little finger movement as possible when changing chords. Certain keys lend themselves well to common-finger combinations. Play through the chords below from left to right.

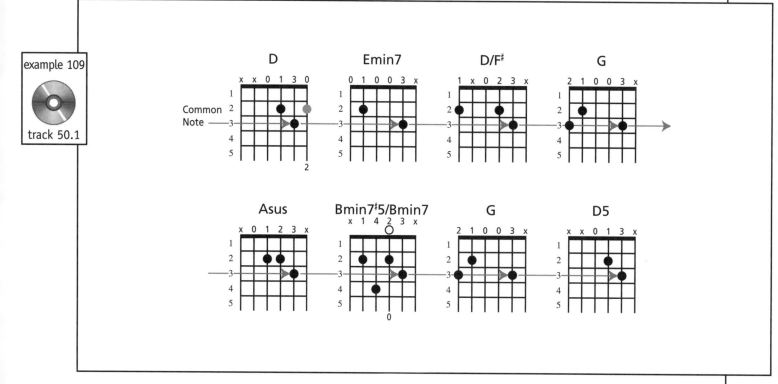

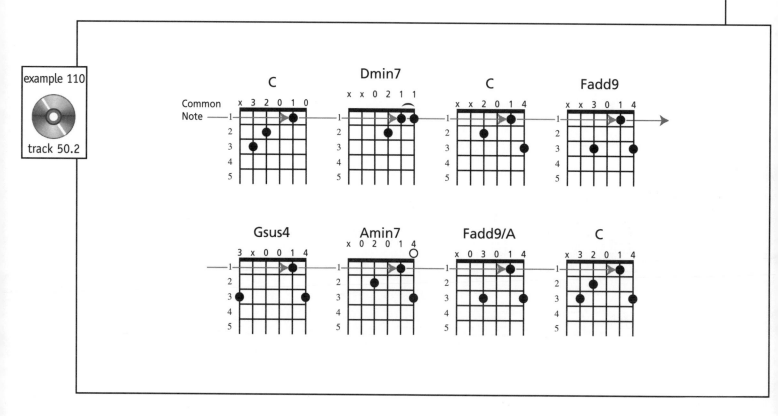

Endings and Cadences

A *cadence* is the ending of a musical phrase, when the music clearly comes to rest. Often, the most clearly noticeable cadence is found at the end of a song. The ending of a song is very important. In fact, a lot of musicians claim that as long as a song's ending is good, the audience will "forgive" the players for any mistakes that might have occured within the song! Here are some ending licks that you might find useful. These examples are in common keys and they lie nicely in (or close to) open chord shapes.

You might find it challenging to sustain the notes in some of the examples. As always, practice them slowly and pay close attention to the rhythms and note durations.

example 112

track 52

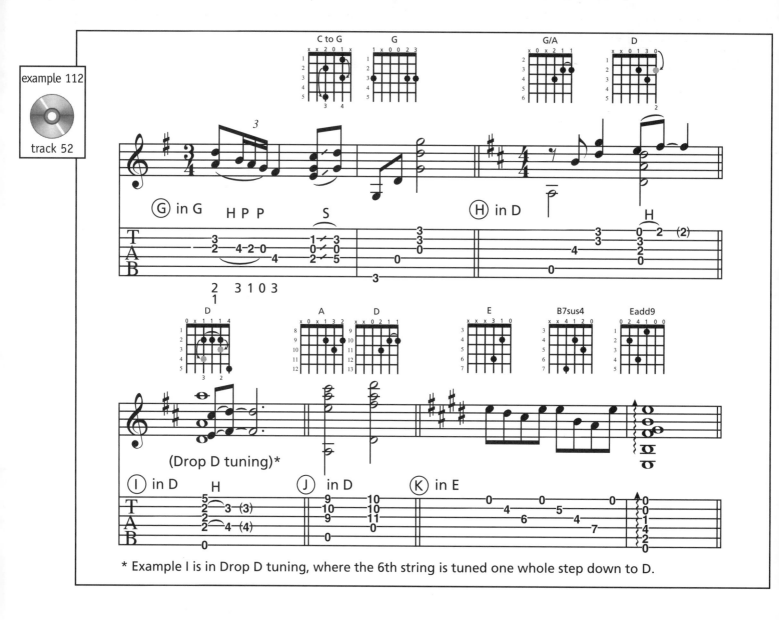

* Example I is in Drop D tuning, where the 6th string is tuned one whole step down to D.

Pedal Tone Diatonic Chord Scales

A familiar sound in many different guitar styles is the sound of the *pedal tone chord scale*. This is a chord scale that has a single bass *pedal* note sustaining while the other chords are moving. These combinations work well if you want movement in your accompaniment but not as much movement in the overall harmony. The following chord scales work whether you are fingerpicking or strumming with a flat pick. The CD that is available for this book gives examples of fingerpicked and strummed versions of each chord scale. As the arrows indicate, strum through the chords from left to right.

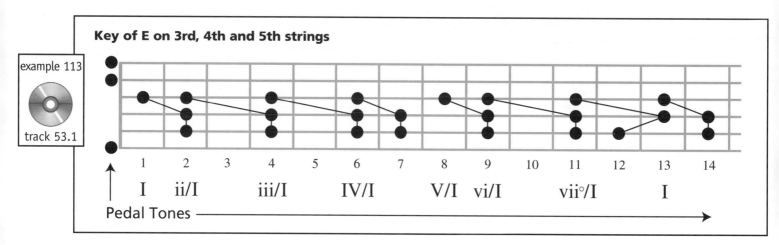

continued on page 69

Key of E on 1st, 2nd and 3rd strings

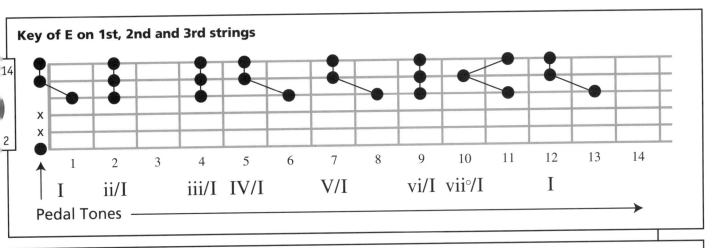

I   ii/I   iii/I IV/I   V/I   vi/I vii°/I   I

Pedal Tones ⟶

Key of A

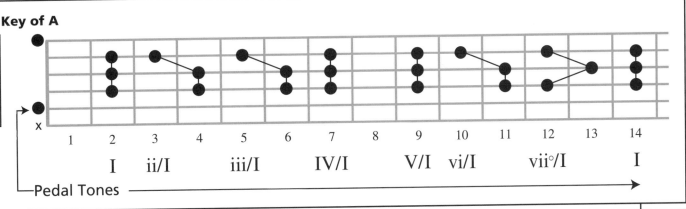

I   ii/I   iii/I   IV/I   V/I vi/I   vii°/I   I

Pedal Tones ⟶

Key of D

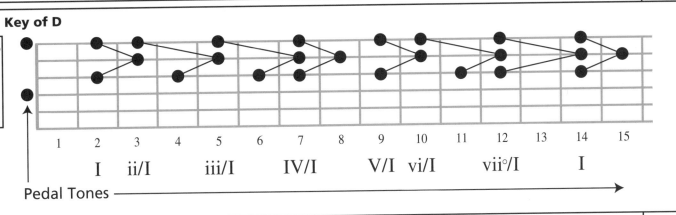

I   ii/I   iii/I   IV/I   V/I vi/I   vii°/I   I

Pedal Tones ⟶

One of the easiest ways to apply pedal notes to your music is to tune your low E string down to the desired pitch. For example, try playing the tonic of the relative minor of the key you are playing in. To do this in E, just tune the low E string down a minor 3rd so that it's now sounding as C♯. Play the chord scale and you will notice that it now has a minor quality.

Relative Minor

Choices of pedal notes in E: E, F♯, G♯, A, B, C♯, D♯

⎣—— *Major Scale* ——⎦

Key of E with C♯ Pedal

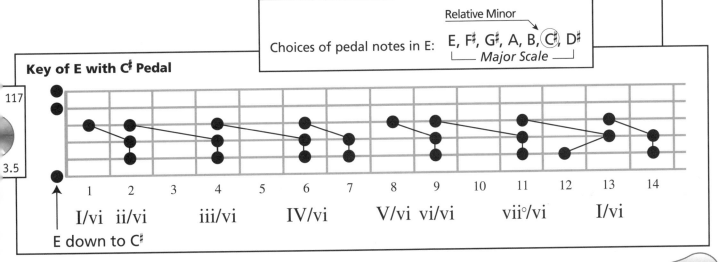

I/vi ii/vi   iii/vi   IV/vi   V/vi vi/vi   vii°/vi   I/vi

E down to C♯

Now experiment by playing each note of the major scale as the pedal note under the moving chord scale. This is a great way to hear the major scale *modes* and their harmonies. When you play a scale starting and ending on something other than the *tonic* (the 1st scale degree), you create a *mode* of the scale. Using the 1st degree of the major scale as a pedal will give you the *Ionian mode*, which has a major sound. Using the 2nd degree gives you the *Dorian* mode, which has a minor sound. Using the 3rd degree gives you the *Phrygian* mode (minor). The 4th is *Lydian* (major). The 5th is *Mixolydian*, which has a dominant 7 sound. The 6th is *Aeolian*, with a relative and natural minor sound. Finally, the 7th pedal note gives you the *Locrian* mode, which is the strangest-sounding mode and has a diminished sound. Notice, by the way, that the harmonic quality of the modes is exactly the same as those of the triads of the major scale: Major, minor, minor, Major, Major, minor and diminished.

Pedal Tone Choices and their Harmony

I	ii	iii	IV	V	vi	vii
Major	minor	minor	Major	Major	minor	half/dim
Ionian	*Dorian*	*Phrygian*	*Lydian*	*Mixolydian*	*Aeolian*	*Locrian*

—————————————— Major Scale ——————————————

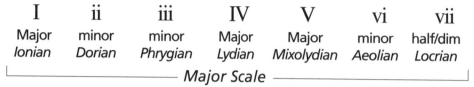

IV - Lydian sound

Choices of pedal notes in A: A, B, C♯, D, E, F♯, G♯

└─ Major Scale ─┘

Key of A with D Pedal

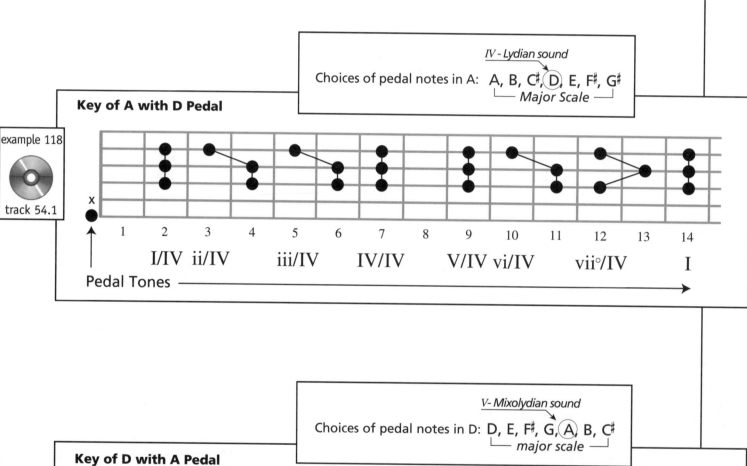

example 118

track 54.1

1 2 3 4 5 6 7 8 9 10 11 12 13 14

I/IV ii/IV   iii/IV   IV/IV   V/IV vi/IV   vii°/IV   I

Pedal Tones ⟶

V - Mixolydian sound

Choices of pedal notes in D: D, E, F♯, G, A, B, C♯

└─ major scale ─┘

Key of D with A Pedal

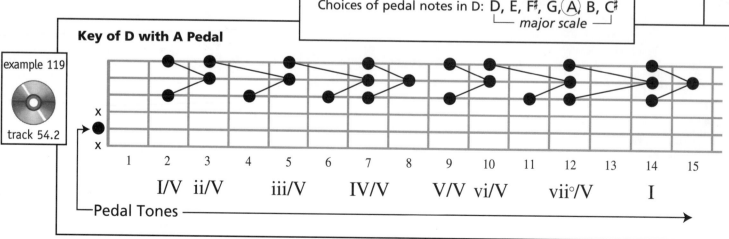

example 119

track 54.2

1 2 3 4 5 6 7 8 9 10 11 12 13 14 15

I/V ii/V   iii/V   IV/V   V/V vi/V   vii°/V   I

Pedal Tones ⟶

As its name implies, an *alternate tuning* is any tuning that differs from the standard E-A-D-G-B-E tuning. When a guitarist plays well in an alternate tuning, it sounds beautiful and seems effortless. Some of the most wonderful sounds to come out of the guitar come from alternate tunings. We will look at the basics of alternate tunings and how to get to them successfully from standard tuning. We will look at the most common: Open D, open G, open C and D-A-D-G-A-D.

The chord scale for each alternate tuning will be shown. This will provide a foundation of chord theory that will get you off and running. Knowing the chord scale will assist you in learning the common chord progressions from familiar songs and in creating your own.

💡 Open D Tuning — D-A-D-F♯-A-D

Tuning to Open D from Standard Tuning:

Step 1: Tune the 6th string down one whole step from low E to low D. Match the harmonic at the 12th fret of the 6th string to the open 4th string.

Step 2: Tune the 3rd string down one half step from G to F♯. Match the open 3rd string to the 4th fret F♯ on the 4th string.

Step 3: Tune the 2nd string down one whole step from B to A. Match the open 2nd string to the harmonic at the 12th fret of the 5th string.

Step 4: Tune the 1st string down one whole step from E to D. Match the open 1st string to the harmonic at the 12th fret of the 4th string.

Open D tuning lends itself to many sounds and styles from the major melodic sound to the blues. Let's start with the beautiful sounding chord scale of D.

D Major Chord Scale in Open D Tuning

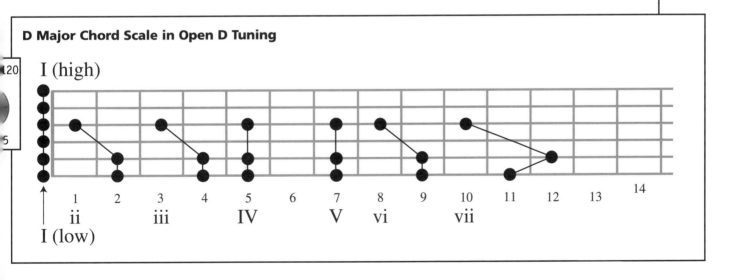

Slide

In *Blues for Ry*, use a *slide*. A slide is a metal or glass tube worn on a left-hand finger. It glides along the strings to create a great blues or country sound. Try it on your 3rd (ring) finger, but not past the second joint. You will then be able to play chords with your other fingers and still keep your thumb behind the neck. To avoid unwanted notes and string noise, use your right hand to mute the strings that aren't being played.

This is a slow piece, so you can take liberties with the tempo, speeding up and slowing down as you wish. This is called *rubato*, which is an Italian word that means "to rob the time" or to take time away from one note and give it to another. This piece works equally well on electric or acoustic guitar. This is a simple Open D Tuning twelve-bar blues in the style of Ry Cooder.

Blues for Ry

8va = Sounds an octave higher than written.

💡 Open G Tuning — D-G-D-G-B-D

From the bottom up, the strings are tuned to the 5th, root, 5th, root, 3rd and 5th of the G Major scale. This tuning has been known and loved by guitarists from the legendary bluesman Robert Johnson to Keith Richards of The Rolling Stones.

Tuning to Open G from Standard Tuning

Step 1: Tune the 6th string down one whole step from low E to low D. Match the harmonic at the 12th fret of the 6th string to the open 4th string.

Step 2: Tune the 5th string down one whole step from A to G. Match the harmonic at the 12th fret of the 5th string to the open 3rd string.

Step 3: Tune the 1st string down a whole step from E to D. Match the open 1st string to the 3rd fret of the 2nd string.

Here is the G Major chord scale in open G tuning. Notice that the chord shapes are identical to those in the open D scale but are moved over one string.

G Major Chord Scale in Open G Tuning

example 121

track 57.1

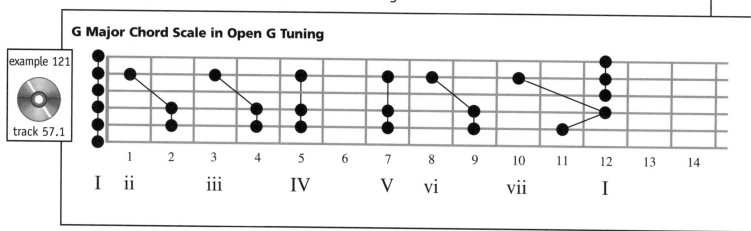

The barre chords below look a lot like the B Minor chord shape. This is a chord shape Keith Richards uses often. Try moving this shape around the fretboard and you'll hear that familiar Rolling Stones sound.

example 122

track 57.2

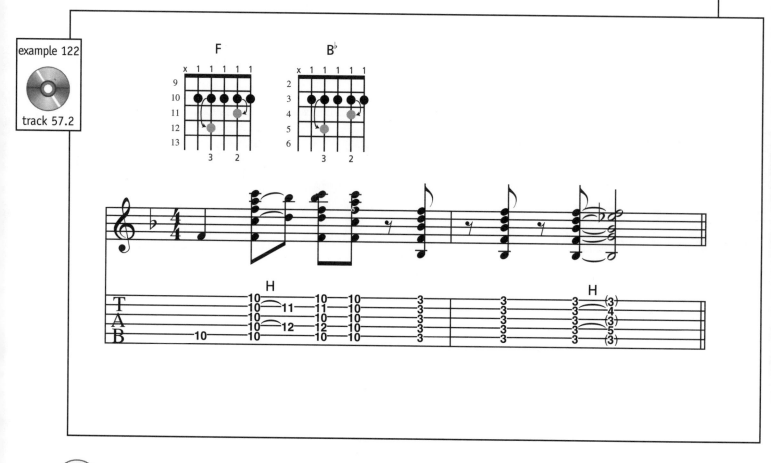

Open C Tuning — C-G-C-G-C-E

From the bottom up, the strings are tuned to the root, 5th, root, 5th, root and 3rd of the C Major scale.

Tuning to Open C from Standard Tuning

Step 1: Tune the 6th string down a Major 3rd from low E to C. Match the harmonic at the 7th fret of the 6th string to the open G on the 3rd string.

Step 2: Tune the 5th string down a whole step from A to G. Match the harmonic at the 5th fret of the 5th string to the harmonic at the 12th fret of the 3rd string.

Step 3: Tune the 4th string down a whole step to C. Match the harmonic at the 12th fret of the 4th string to the harmonic at the 5th fret of the 6th string.

Step 4: Tune the 2nd string up a half step to C. Match the open 2nd string to the harmonic at the 12th fret of the 4th string.

This tuning is cool because its bass notes are so low! Shown below are two chord scales. The first one has the same shape as the D and G chord scales moved up one more string to the 4th, 3rd and 1st strings. The second is a lower octave chord scale that takes advantage of the lower bass notes. Singer/songwriter David Wilcox uses open C tuning in songs such as *Eye of the Hurricane* and *Block Dog*.

C Major Chord Scale in Open C Tuning (1st, 3rd and 4th Strings)

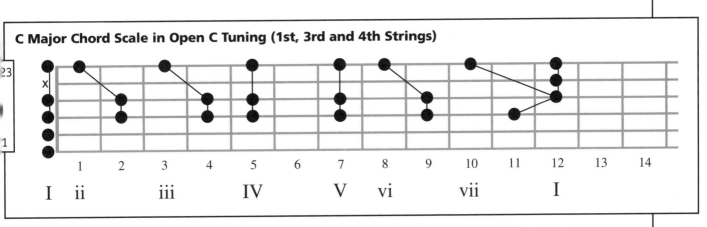

C Major Chord Scale in Open C Tuning (4th, 5th and 6th Strings)

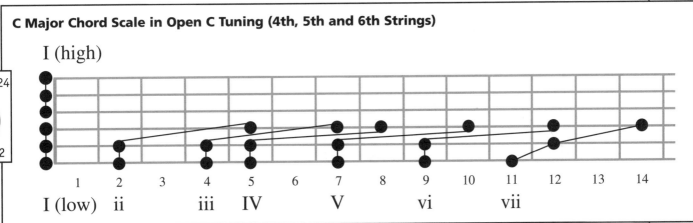

Optional Chord Shapes (in C Tuning)

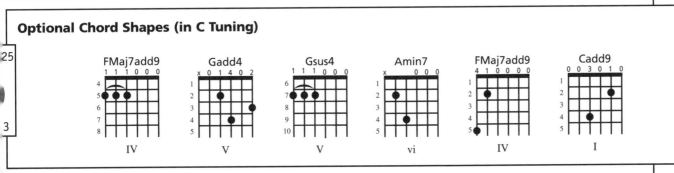

There are many great-sounding variations on this tuning. An interesting one is to drop the high E down to D. Martin Simpson is well known for playing in C-G-C-G-C-D tuning on songs like his *Donal Og/My Generous Lover* or *Hard Love*.

It is also very effective to use a capo in these open tunings. If you play the following piece with a capo on the 1st fret, you'll be playing in the beautiful and unusual key of D♭. Try it! That's how the song was recorded for the CD that is available for this book.

The Hope Song (Etude for Open C Tuning)

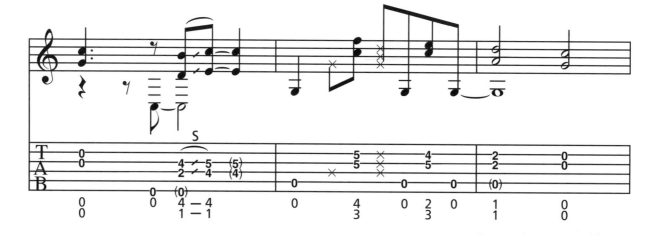

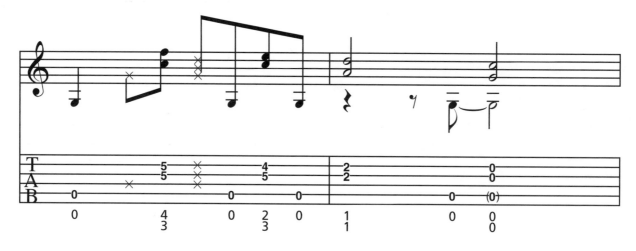

💡 D-A-D-G-A-D Tuning

From bottom to top, the strings are D (root), A (5th), D (root), G (4th), A (5th) and D (root).

Tuning to D-A-D-G-A-D from Standard Tuning

Step 1: Tune the 6th string down one whole step from low E to low D. Match the harmonic at the 12th fret of the 6th string to the open 4th string.

Step 2: Tune the 2nd string down one whole step from B to A. Match the harmonic at the 12th fret of the 5th string to the open 2nd string.

Step 3: Tune the 1st string down one whole step from E to D. Match the open 1st string to the harmonic at the 12th fret of the 4th string.

D-A-D-G-A-D is one of the most popular open tunings. It is well known for its beautiful Celtic sound (music of the British Isles) and it lends itself to easy chord positions. Pierre Bensusan and Lawrence Juber are just two of the many great guitarists who use the D-A-D-G-A-D tuning. D-A-D-G-A-D sounds great with a capo. Try using one when you practice these exercises.

Here is the chord scale in D Major in D-A-D-G-A-D:

(Because the chords are all in roughly the same area of the neck, they are shown in diagrams, rather than ascending the neck as on the previous pages.)

example 126

track 60.1

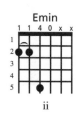 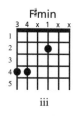 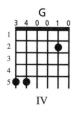 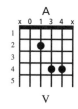 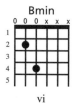 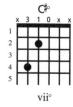

Here are optional fingerings for the D and A chords:

example 127

track 60.2

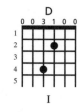 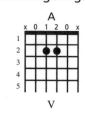

For more alternate tuning resources, check out:

Introducing Alternate Tunings, by Mark Dziuba
March 1999, Acoustic Guitar Magazine
www.acousticguitar.com
www.jonimitchell.com
www.davidwilcox.com
www.stropes.com

what's next?

We hope you have enjoyed this exploration of chord playing. Don't stop now! There's lots more to learn. Get a good chord encyclopedia and learn as many new chords as you can. Here is a list of just a few books about chords (Alfred item numbers are included for your convenience):

Basix™—Guitar Chord Dictionary ....#16750

Chord Connections ....#16754

Guitar Chord Encyclopedia ....#4432

Guitar Chord Progression Encyclopedia ...#17868

Alfred's Basic Guitar Chord Chart.............#14899